D0121760

Soccer
Drills

A Guide for all Levels of Ability

David Smith

The Crowood Press

First published in 2012 by
The Crowood Press Ltd
Ramsbury, Marlborough
Wiltshire SN8 2HR

www.crowood.com

British Library Cataloguing-in-Publication Data
A catalogue record for this book is available from the British Library.

ISBN 978 1 84797 356 6

Acknowledgements
Firstly, I would like to thank the excellent soccer coaches I have had the privilege of working with and who have helped in the development of ideas for this book, especially Steve 'Melt' Elliott, Michael 'Buffalo Bill' Hillary, Simon 'Big Mac' Wilby, Kelvin 'Mouse' Dawson and Michael Laidler.

Secondly, to my lovely wife and son for their support and patience whilst writing this book and for having to wait around and amuse themselves as I coached three-hour sessions, sometimes twice a day, on soccer fields around Harrisburg, Pennsylvania.

Also many thanks must go to the fantastic Matthews, Wilson and Lamb families for showing us such great hospitality and keeping us entertained, over many summers of coaching in the United States.

For helping to produce this book I am very grateful for the help and guidance of Hannah Shakespeare and all the other staff at The Crowood Press who have contributed to its publication.

Then there are the countless number of parents and volunteers who give up their time to run teams and recreational soccer programmes on both sides of the Atlantic, without whom children would not have the wonderful opportunities that they do to experience and enjoy this beautiful game.

Finally, I give my thanks to all the staff in schools I have had the pleasure of working alongside over the years, who have provided invaluable feedback when trying out my new ideas.

Soccer drill diagrams created using Soccer Playbook 010, by Jes-Soft.

Front cover photo and back cover bottom image © iStockphoto.com/srickke
Back cover top image © iStockphoto.com/kycstudio
Back cover middle image © Shawn Pecor/Shutterstock.com

Originated by The Manila Typesetting Company

Printed and bound in Singapore by Craft Print International

Contents

Introduction

Contained within this book are 190 quality soccer drills, each with three or more diagrams and step-by-step instructions to make them easy to follow. Most of these also conclude with suggestions as to how you could change the numbers, organization, or level of challenge, to make them suitable for almost any group you may find yourself coaching.

What makes this book special is that they are organized into chapters, using similar playing areas, to make it easier for you to plan fun, clearly focused sessions, with a minimum amount of time, effort and organization. If you're quite new to coaching, then suggestions have been made at the beginning of each chapter as to how the drills could be combined to create different sessions. If you are an experienced coach, or once you become more familiar with the drills, you can just dip in and use particular activities that you like, or mix and match them to suit your own coaching needs or requirements.

If you're a Physical Education teacher like myself, or even if you just find yourself teaching one or two lessons of this subject a week, then this book also offers a great source of quick and easy-to-use ideas, suitable for all age groups. The great thing is that it doesn't matter whether you're teaching basketball, netball, rugby, hockey, cricket, rounders or even altlhetics. This fantastic collection of activities can be used to provide warm-ups, skill practise and fun games to liven up your lessons, whilst still meeting the requirements of the National Curriculum.

CHAPTER 1

Large Area Drills – Beginners

Although aimed at those new to soccer, the great thing about this first collection of drills, is their accessibility and sense of fun for all levels of ability. With the purpose of achieving maximum participation, they only require a basic level of equipment, an open area of ground and any number of players.

They are carefully designed to act as a great vehicle for promoting the essential basic skills required to begin the mastery of a soccer ball. Athletic development is promoted by focusing on activities that demand co-ordination, balance, speed and agility. Developing techniques such as dribbling, running with the ball, turning, receiving and passing, is achieved by combining the need for both repetition and practise, within a functional, game-type environment.

All you need to do is mark out a rectangular area of a suitable size for the age and ability of your group. The smaller the space, the better the level of skill and control required from the players. Then, select and combine the drills to suit your purpose and enjoy session after session of fun, whilst ensuring your players get the best possible start they could have to their soccer learning journey.

POSSIBLE SESSIONS

The following selections are only suggestions of how drills could be combined to create a one, or two-hour session. As a teacher or coach, you need to assess the ability of your group and take into account possible numbers before making appropriate choices of your own. All these sessions could also be started with a warm-up of your own and ended with some regular, small-sided games.

- High Five
- Skittle Ball
- Pirates and Buccaneers

- Traffic Jam
- Body Parts Dribble
- What time is it Mr Wolf?
- Star Wars
- Defend the Castle

- Animal Safari
- Cone Signals
- Dribble Pursuit

- Locked in the Stocks
- Cone Gates Passing
- Guardians of the Cones 2
- Through the Gate
- Cone Gate Game

ANIMAL SAFARI

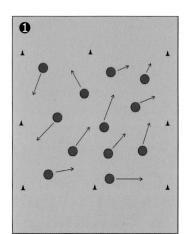

How it works

❶ All players jog/run around inside the playing area, trying to stay in space. The coach calls out the name of an animal and the players copy the following actions:

- Kangaroo – upright bounce from two feet to two feet;
- Snake – crawl around on the stomach;
- Cheetah – sprint around as fast as they can;
- Frog – crouching, bounce from two feet to two feet;
- Camel – on hands and feet with backside high in the air;
- Crab – move sideways on hands and feet with stomach facing upwards;
- Eagle – run and swoop with arms spread out;
- Penguin – waddle with both feet close together.

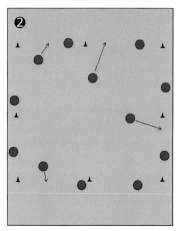

❷ Lion, (or coach), makes a roaring noise – all players run away to stand around the edge of the playing area before being caught by the lion, (coach).

❸ Players now dribble a ball and copy the following actions:

- Kangaroo – upright bounce with the ball gripped between the feet;
- Snake – crawl around pushing the ball forward with the head;
- Cheetah – sprint whilst keeping control of the ball;
- Frog – crouching bounce with the ball gripped between the knees;
- Camel – on hands and feet with backside high in the air and the ball stuck up the back of the shirt;
- Crab – moving sideways on hands and feet with stomach facing upwards, kicking the ball with the outside of the feet;
- Eagle – swoop with arms out whilst dribbling the ball;
- Penguin – quick touches between the insides of the feet;
- Lion, (or coach), makes a roaring noise – all players dribble to the edge of the playing area and stop the ball with their foot on top, before being caught/tackled by the lion, (coach).

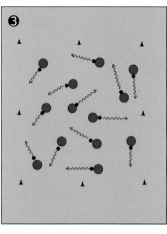

Possible changes

- Make up some of your own 'Animal Safari' actions.

ARE WE THERE YET?

How it works

❶All players jog/run around inside the playing area trying to stay in space. On a signal from the coach, all the players must stop and say/shout: 'Are we there yet?' The coach replies: 'No, go and...' giving the players an instruction for an action or task such as:

- do five sit-ups;
- run around a cone;
- do ten star jumps;
- give everyone a high five.

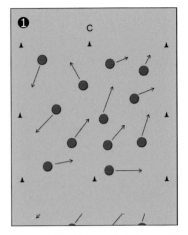

Or any other action/task you want to give them, (the sillier, the better). As soon as they have followed the instruction, they continue to jog/run around inside the playing area.

❷Eventually, after several actions, when the players ask the question, the coach answers: 'Yes'. At this point, all the players must try to chase and tag the coach. First one to tag the coach wins. (If you don't fancy being chased, get the players to run to a certain place, or coned area, and the first player to get there wins).

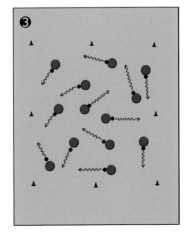

❸Repeat, but dribbling a ball this time and giving players different instructions such as:

- do twenty toe taps on top of the ball with alternate feet;
- dribble around a cone;
- do twenty touches between the inside of the feet with the ball;
- dribble around giving everyone a high five;
- throw the ball up in the air and catch it five times.

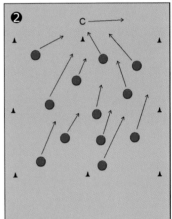

Or any other action/task you want to give them, (the sillier, the better).

Eventually, after several actions, when the players ask the question, the coach answers: 'Yes'. Players must then leave their ball to chase and tag the coach as before.

MR BEAN'S BEANS

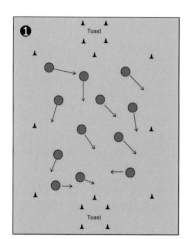

How it works

❶This idea originally came from a gymnastics warm-up on a P.E. website, and then I started to add in a few of my own bean instructions that were more suitable for a soccer warm-up. Each player jogs/runs around inside the playing area, looking to stay in space. The coach then shouts out different types of beans and the players have to do the following actions:

- Jumping Bean – jump around two feet to two feet;
- Baked Bean – lie down on the ground and sunbathe;
- Jelly Bean – stop and wobble like a jelly;
- Broad Bean – stop with arms and legs stretched out wide;
- String Bean – stop with legs together and arms straight up;
- Mr Bean – sit down and pretend to drive a Mini.

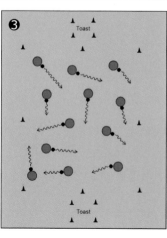

❷Beans on toast – run to sit down inside either of the coned spaces, (toast), at each end of the playing area. Plus any others you might like to make up yourself.

❸Players dribble a ball around, the coach shouts out different types of beans and the players have to do the following actions:

- Jumping Bean – jump with the ball between the feet;
- Baked Bean – lie down and sunbathe using the ball as a pillow;
- Jelly Bean – stop and wobble like a jelly;
- Broad Bean – stop with arms and legs stretched out wide;
- String Bean – stop as before with the ball held over their head;
- Mr Bean – sit down on the ball and pretend to drive a Mini;
- Beans on Toast – dribble the ball to sit down on either piece of toast.

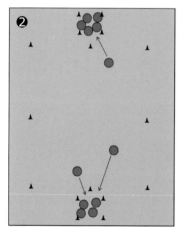

Possible changes

- Once they are familiar with the instructions, you could start giving each player a letter of the word B E A N every time they make a mistake, or if they are the last one to follow the instruction correctly.

CONE SIGNALS

How it works

❶ Players have a ball each and dribble around inside the playing area, keeping control of the ball and their heads up. The coach holds up a coloured cone and the players have to perform the skill that matches that cone. The coach may need to introduce these one at a time and allow players time to practise.

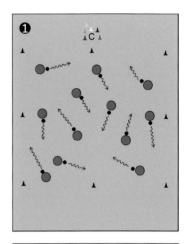

❷ Here are a few suggestions for skills/instructions:

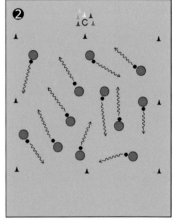

- Green – players dribble freely around the playing area;
- Red – players stop and put their foot on the ball;
- Orange – players touch the ball between insteps of both feet without moving;
- White – players sit on the ball;
- Blue – players pick up the ball and hold it above their head;
- Yellow – players use their left foot only.

The possibilities are endless. If you don't have many different coloured cones then use signals, or hold up a ball for one skill, a cone for another, wave a bib/pinny for another and so on.

❸ **Possible changes**

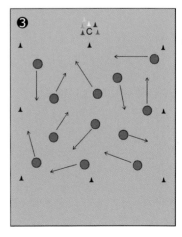

- Do it without a ball first, as part of a warm-up, but just alter the instructions for each coloured cone to actions such as:
- Green – run/jog freely around the playing area;
- Red – players stop;
- Orange – players stop and jog on the spot;
- White – players run around a cone;
- Blue – players run and jump up as if to head a ball;
- Yellow – players stop and lie down.

MR MEN PARTY

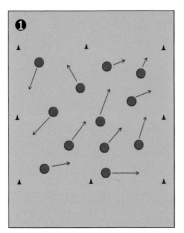

How it works

❶ All players jog/run around inside the playing area, trying to stay in space. The coach calls out any, or all, of these Mr Men characters arriving at the party and the players perform the following actions:

- ■ Mr Rush – players run quickly around the playing area;
- ■ Mr Slow – players move in slow motion;
- ■ Mr Lazy – fall to the ground and lie down as if asleep;
- ■ Mr Bump – players must gently bump shoulders with another player;
- ■ Mr Small – crouch down into a small ball;
- ■ Mr Bounce – bounce up and down on the spot, or whilst moving around the playing area;
- ■ Mr Mischief – try to tag someone else without being tagged.

The coach could make a signal for the players to return to a normal run/jog around the playing area, or could just call out Mr Jog.

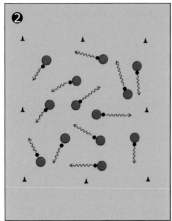

❷ Players now dribble a ball and copy the following actions:

- ■ Mr Rush – players dribble quickly around the playing area;
- ■ Mr Slow – players dribble in slow motion;
- ■ Mr Lazy – stop the ball and lie down, as if asleep, using the ball as a pillow;
- ■ Mr Bump – players must bump balls with as many other players as possible;
- ■ Mr Small – sit on the ball all curled up;
- ■ Mr Bounce – bounce the ball up and down on the spot, or whilst moving around the playing area;
- ■ Mr Mischief – try to kick someone else's ball out of the playing area, without losing their own.

The coach could make a signal for the players to return to a normal dribble around the playing area, or could just call out Mr Jog.

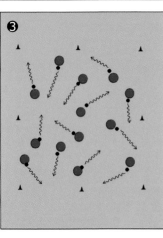

❸ Possible changes

- ■ There are many more Mr Men names you could think up actions for, or have a Little Miss party instead.

PIRATE SHIP

How it works

❶All players jog/run around inside the playing area, (on board the pirate ship) trying to stay in space. The coach calls out any, or all, of these pirate instructions and the players perform the following actions:

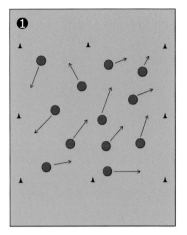

- ■ Port – all the players run to the left side of the ship;
- ■ Starboard – players run to the right side of the ship;
- ■ Bow – all the players run to the front of the ship;
- ■ Stern – all the players run to the back of the ship;
- ■ Land Ahoy – all the players run to any side of the ship and look out, or pretend to use a telescope;
- ■ Hit the Deck – fall to the ground and lie down;
- ■ Scrub the Decks – kneel down and pretend to scrub;
- ■ Shark Attack – coach runs in to try and catch pirates and throw them overboard, or make them walk the plank;
- ■ Captain on Deck – all the players stop, salute and shout: 'Aye Aye Cap'n'.

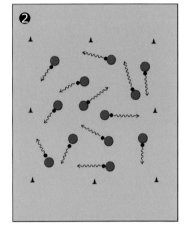

❷Players now dribble a ball and copy the following actions:

- ■ Port – all the players dribble to the left side of the ship;
- ■ Starboard – players dribble to the right side of the ship;
- ■ Bow – all the players dribble to the front of the ship;
- ■ Stern – all the players dribble to the back of the ship;
- ■ Land Ahoy – all the players dribble to any side of the ship and look out, or pretend to use a telescope;
- ■ Hit the Deck – fall to the ground and lie down;
- ■ Scrub the Decks – roll foot over the ball forwards and backwards and side to side;
- ■ Shark Attack – coach runs in to try and tackle pirates, kicking their ball over the side of the ship and shouting: 'Man overboard';
- ■ Captain on Deck – all the players stop with their foot on top of the ball, salute and shout 'Aye Aye Cap'n'.

❸ ■ Man the cannons – all players dribble to either side of the ship and put their foot on the ball;

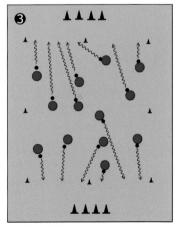

- ■ Fire – players pass/shoot their ball to try and sink the two ships, (rows of tall cones), on either side.

Possible changes

- ■ Have a go at making up some of your own pirate instructions with different actions.

TRAFFIC JAM

How it works

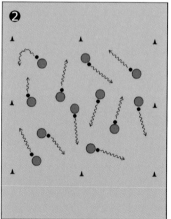

❶ Each player stands in a space in the playing area with a ball each. They must steer their car, (ball), safely around the playing area, (road), without losing control. Players have to follow instructions called out by the coach, starting with:

- Green – players dribble around inside the playing area;
- Red – players stop and put their foot on the ball;
- Amber – players touch the ball between the insteps of both feet without moving;
- Turn – steer their car, (ball), to move in a different direction.

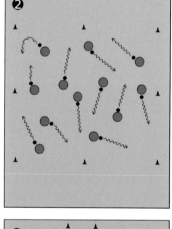

❷ You can also introduce gears whilst in green dribbling mode:

- First gear – slow jog;
- Second gear – steady run;
- Third gear – quicker run;
- Fourth gear – quickest run.

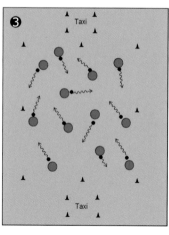

❸ As players get familiar with those instructions, you could add these in as well:

- Crash – all the players must fall to the ground and scream in pain, then quickly get up and carry on. (Only call if two or more players allow their cars to collide). The two players who crashed must go to the mechanic, (coach), to have their car fixed, which means standing out for twenty or thirty seconds.
- Runaway Truck – the coach comes into the playing area and crashes into any cars, (balls), that are not being kept under control. Kick the ball out of the playing area and the players have to go and fetch it and return as quickly as possible.
- Taxi – players have to leave their car and run to get into the taxi, (two coned off areas outside each end of the playing area).

BATMAN AND ROBIN

How it works

❶ Players stand in pairs within a large playing area. One of the pair must be Batman, wearing a coloured bib/pinny, whilst their partner must be Robin. On the call of 'Batman' from the coach, the red players start jogging/running and the yellow players, (Robin), must follow closely. At any time the coach can call 'Robin', and the partners change quickly to Batman following Robin.

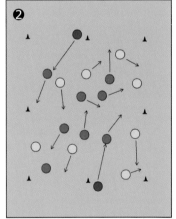

❷ After a short while the coach can make the call of 'Joker', at which time the two blue players, (Jokers), run into the playing area. They can tag any Batman or Robin, and that player must stand still with a big smile on their face. They can be freed only by a tag from their partner. Play can continue until the last pair has been caught. This pair are the winners and can become the Jokers in another game. Alternatively, a set time can be allowed and the winners are any pair with both players still free after one or two minutes. If there are no pairs free, then the winners are any partners with one character still free.

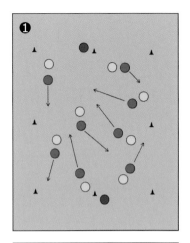

❸ All the players now have a ball and follow each other whilst dribbling the ball, depending on the call of Batman or Robin from the coach. When the Jokers, (blue players), are called in, they must try to tackle and win possession of a ball from any of the other players and then kick it out of the playing area. The Batman or Robin who has been tackled can try and win possession back from the Joker, until the ball is out of the playing area.

When a Batman or a Robin has had their ball kicked out, they can help their partner keep possession of their ball by being available for a pass. Play can continue until the last pair has lost possession of a ball. This pair are the winners and can become the Jokers in another game. Alternatively, a set time can be allowed and the winners are the pair with both, or one ball, still in play after one or two minutes.

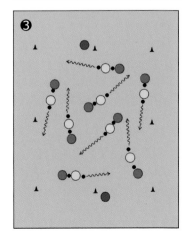

Possible changes

■ The Jokers could be any of the Batman and Robin villains such as: the Penguin, Catwoman or Poison Ivy, who puts players to sleep when tagged. They can then only be revived by a touch from their own Batman or Robin partner.

DRIBBLE PURSUIT

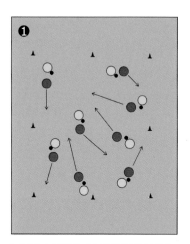

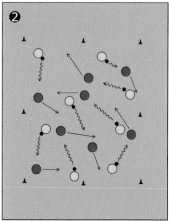

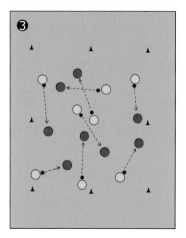

How it works

❶ Players stand in pairs within a large playing area. Every yellow player has a ball at their feet. On a signal from the coach, the red players run away from their yellow partner to try and get as far away from them as possible, but must stay within the playing area.

❷ Yellow players must dribble the ball and stay as close to their partner as possible. All players must keep their heads up to avoid collisions and watch out for their partners. Red players can use other players in the grid as a screen/obstruction to make it harder for their partner to follow.

After twenty or thirty seconds, the coach gives another signal and all the players must stop as quickly as possible. (Try to do this when the players are fairly well spread out).

❸ Move players back if they continue running after the signal. The red players then turn to face their partners and position their legs so that they are wide open. The yellow players must try to pass the ball between their partner's legs, so the closer together they are, the better. (This may need to be done one pair at a time because, as shown in the diagram, the paths of the passes may sometimes cross each other).

Yellow players get three points for passing the ball through the red player's legs, and one point if the ball hits the leg of the red player. Players stand back together and swap roles, so that the red players are now pursuing the yellow players. Play several rounds and keep a running total of scores, partner versus partner, or red team versus yellow team.

ELECTRIC EEL

How it works
❶ The yellow players, (electric eels), have to try and tag the red players, (fish), as they run across the open area, (sea).

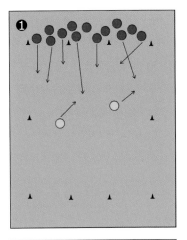

❷ If the red players are tagged, then they are stunned and must stand still, wherever they are caught. The red players are only safe when they get to the other side of the area, without being tagged. Repeat with the red players trying to get back across the area, whilst being chased by the electric eels. Stunned fish can also now tag other red players as they run past, but can only pivot on one foot. Continue until the last fish is caught. The size of the area, and the number of electric eels at the start, will depend on your group size.

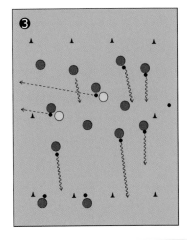

❸ This time the players, (fish), have to dribble their ball across, while the electric eels have to kick the balls out of the area to stun the fish. Stunned fish can also kick out stray balls from other red players if they don't keep them under control, but again can only pivot on one foot.

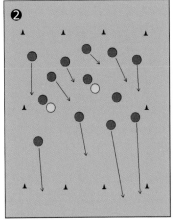

BOB DOWN TAG

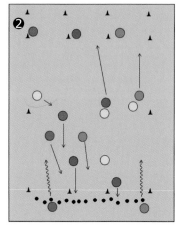

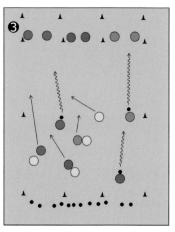

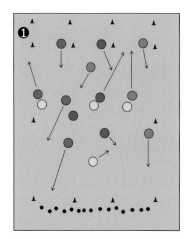

How it works

❶ The yellow players are the taggers, and the other three teams are the runners. The runners stand together in a channel, at the opposite end of the playing area to a line of balls. On a signal from the coach, all the players from each team try to run to the other end without being tagged. Yellow players must tag a runner to send them back to the start.

However, if a runner bobs down, (crouches down), before being tagged, they are allowed to stay in the game, but at some point must try to get up and continue. Taggers are not allowed to stand right next to a runner who has bobbed down, but must chase after another runner. In this diagram, three players have been tagged and must go back to the start to wait for the next round. Some players have nearly made it through to the other end without being tagged.

❷ This diagram shows that two more runners have been caught and must return to the start. If a runner gets to the other end, as the red and green players have done, they must try to dribble a ball back to the start. Yellow players must still tag runners to send them back to the start. However, if a runner with a ball bobs down and sits on the ball before being tagged, they are allowed to stay in the game, but at some point must try to get up and continue. As before, taggers are not allowed to stand right next to a runner who has bobbed down and sat on a ball, but must chase after another runner.

❸ Play continues until all the runners have either been caught or got back to the start with a ball. The winners are the team that gets the most balls back to the start, after a set number of rounds.

Possible changes

■ Play three or four rounds with the same team tagging, or rotate the teams in each round, so that they all take it in turns to be the taggers.

■ If runners are finding it difficult to get back with a ball, just have two of the tagging team in play, whilst the other two rest, and then switch for the next round.

■ Taggers could be made to tackle players on the way back, to kick the ball out of the playing area.

OVER THE HEDGE

How it works

❶ The red team, (animals from the movie), have to try and go 'Over the Hedge' by running to the far end of the playing area, without being tagged, to get a ball, (food). The yellow players, (cats), must try to stop them by tagging them on the way across.

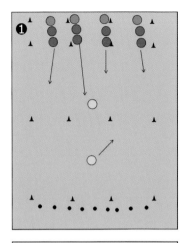

❷ If tagged, the red players must return to the start. If not tagged, the red players try to dribble a ball back across the playing area. The yellow players then try to tackle the ball and kick it out of the playing area. They must each stay in their zone and not cross the middle of the playing area. Players must stop the ball within the coned area on their return, in order for it to count. They must be in control of the ball, and not just kick it over the line from a long way back. Teams compete against each other over three to four rounds, to try and bring the most food back 'Over the Hedge.'

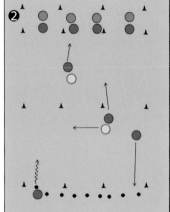

❸ **Possible changes**
  ■ If a player is tagged on the way across, they could stand at the side of the playing area and be available for a pass, to help their team-mates keep possession.
  ■ If a player's ball is tackled and kicked out, they could also support team-mates by being available for passes, in order to get the food back safely.

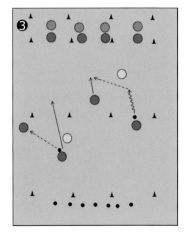

BALL RAIDERS

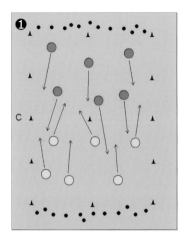

How it works

❶ Two teams start inside adjacent squares, with lots of balls spread across each end of the playing area. On a signal from the coach, the players must run across the other team's square to get a ball. They can then dribble a ball back across the playing area, stopping it behind the cones at their end.

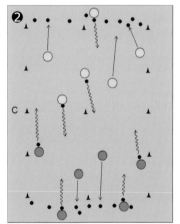

❷ The players then run back again to see if they can dribble another ball back. No players are allowed to tackle, but if a player loses control of a ball and it goes outside the playing area, then it is lost for that round. Play for one or two minutes, then stop and count up the number of balls at each end to work out the winning team. Alternatively, the teams could score as follows:

- three points for a ball stopped at their end of the playing area;
- two points for a ball being dribbled back and inside their square;
- one point for a ball being dribbled back, but inside the other team's square.

Play several rounds and keep a running total of the scores.

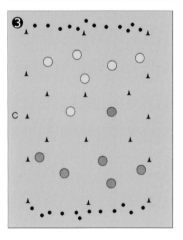

❸ Possible changes

- Set up a central zone with cones and have one player, (or more, depending on group numbers), from each team who must stay inside that area. Play again, but this time the players in the central zone are allowed to tackle players from the other team. They are only allowed to tackle in that area. If they win a ball in the tackle, they can pass it to one of their own team. That player can then dribble the ball to stop it behind the cones at their end of the playing area. Keep scores, and change the players in the middle for the start of a new round.

BOMBS AWAY

How it works
❶ Two teams start inside adjacent squares with lots of balls, (bombs), spread around. A third team stands around the outside of the two squares.

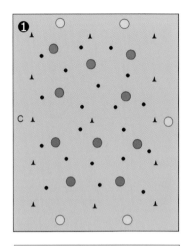

❷ On a signal from the coach, the players try to pass as many balls as they can into the other team's square. The yellow team and the coach can pass any balls back in that come out of the playing area. Play for one minute, then stop and count up the number of balls, (bombs), in each square to work out the winning team.

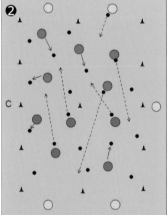

❸ Swap the yellow team with one of the other teams and then play again. Repeat until all of the teams have played against each other.

Possible changes
- The players have to pick up a ball and feed it to one of their team-mates to head, or side-foot volley, into the opponent's playing area.
- Place a large cone in the centre of each grid area. If a player hits the big cone of another team with a pass, they get one or two bombs knocked off their score at the end of the game.

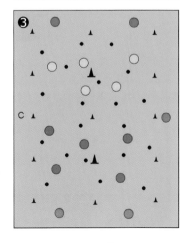

WHAT TIME IS IT MR WOLF?

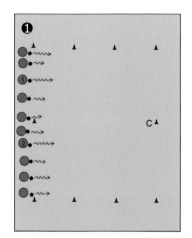

How it works

❶ This drill is an old playground favourite and makes for a fun game that all young players will enjoy. Players all space out at one side of the playing area, with a ball at their feet, while the coach, (Mr Wolf), stands at the other side. On a signal from the coach, the players start dribbling across the area, keeping the ball close to their feet.

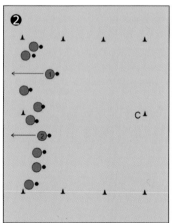

❷ At any time the coach can quickly turn around to face the group. Any player who doesn't have their foot on the ball within a count of three, two, one, has to go back to the beginning to start again, as with Red Players one and two in the diagram. All the children then call out together 'What time is it Mr Wolf?' The wolf replies with a time of day such as: 'It's two 'o' clock' or 'It's eleven 'o' clock'. The coach then turns back around and the players start to dribble again. Repeat this several times with the players gradually getting closer and closer.

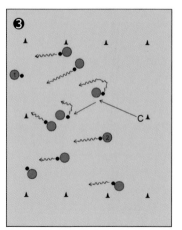

❸ As the players get closer, the coach, (wolf), when asked what time it is, can say: 'It's dinner time!' Players then have to turn and dribble their ball back to the start as quickly as possible, while the coach tries to run after, catch and 'gobble up' as many players as possible before they can get back to safety.

Possible changes

■ For older, more skilful players, the coach can call out: 'head', 'knee' or 'foot'. Each player then has to control the ball with that part of the body and catch it. If they succeed, the players can take one stride forward towards the wolf. If the wolf turns around and a player has dropped the ball, or is taking more than one stride, then they must return to the start.

BODY PARTS DRIBBLE

How it works

❶ Pairs of players start at one side of a large playing area. Player Ones dribble the ball out to the far side of the playing area and perform a turn, before dribbling back to stop the ball on the starting line for their partner.

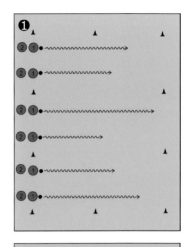

❷ Player Twos then repeat this, performing the same turn. After a few turns for each player, the coach can demonstrate a different type of turn for the players to perform. The players repeat this dribble and turn sequence, using the new turning technique. Turning techniques could include:

- drag back turn;
- inside/outside of the foot cut;
- Cruyff turn.

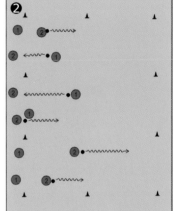

❸ As players continue, the coach can then shout out body parts and, whoever is dribbling the ball at that time, has to stop and place that body part on the ball as quickly as possible. Make sure players use their feet to stop the ball and not their hands. On a signal from the coach, players then carry on.

Possible changes

- Players could stop the ball, level with the middle cone, on the way back to their partner and pass.
- Players could stop the ball as above, pick it up, and then feed the ball for their partner to control, before dribbling across to the other side.

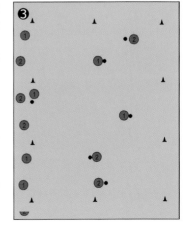

COCONUT SHY

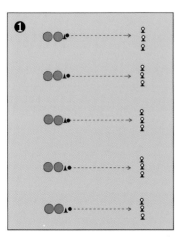

How it works

❶ Three cones are placed opposite each pair of players, with a ball balanced on the top of each one, (the coconut shy). To win the game the players must knock all three balls off the cones within two minutes. In order to do this, the first player passes towards the balls balanced on the cones.

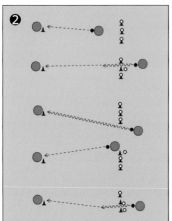

❷ Hit or miss, the player must then run out to get the ball back to their partner as quickly as possible, (running with the ball or passing). Players have two minutes to try and knock all three balls off the cones.

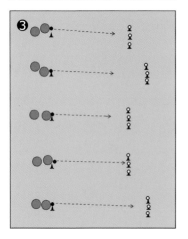

❸ Possible changes
- You could have teams of three with a larger group.
- Play again, but if a pair/group is successful, then move the cones a bit further away to make it harder, (as shown in the diagram), for the next round.
- Keep the balls at the same distance, but gradually reduce the time allowed to knock them off.

DEFEND THE CASTLE

How it works

❶ Two yellow players defend the four cone goals, (castle), at one end of a large playing area. The other two yellow players stand outside the playing area, but swap in for the next team. On a signal from the coach, the red players must try and dribble their balls across the playing area and through one of the cone gates.

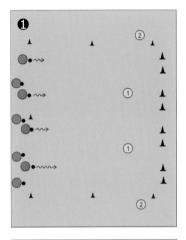

❷ The two yellow players attempt to win a ball and kick it out of the playing area. If it is not kicked out, then the red player can retrieve the ball and carry on. If their ball is kicked out, then that red player can support other players in their team.

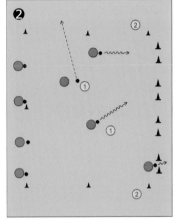

❸ When the red team have finished, they dribble their ball, or jog back to the start, around the outside of the playing area. Yellow Player Ones swap places with the Yellow Player Twos, to defend the castle. The blue team can then try and repeat the same mission as the red team.

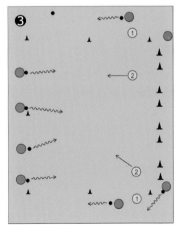

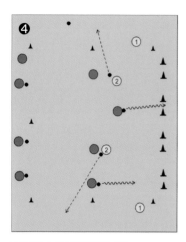

❹ Two blue players have had their balls kicked out in this round, so the blue team will start the next round with only two balls between them.

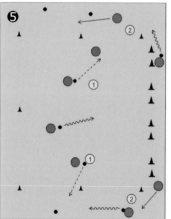

❺ When the red team start for a second time, only three of the players begin with a ball, as one of them was kicked out during the last round. The fourth player still offers their support for a pass, if another red player is pressured by a yellow defender. The red and blue teams compete to keep hold of at least one ball, for as many rounds as possible.

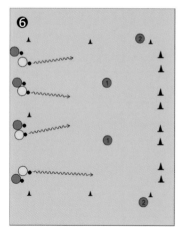

❻ Rotate the teams, so that each different colour become the defenders, (this time the red team), and start the game again. Each team should compete against each other, and the defenders should also try and beat the team record of how well they can defend the castle.

Possible changes
- You can play this game with larger numbers, but an even amount of players on each team works better when you swap the defenders for each round.
- Play with all four defenders protecting the castle, if you need to increase the level of challenge.

HIGH FIVE

How it works

❶ Two teams stand next to each other in pairs. The coach gives the following instructions for players to follow:

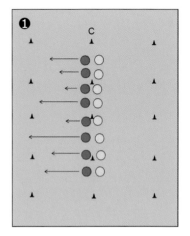

1. the red team runs to the edge of the playing area and back to the middle;
2. the yellow team runs to the edge of the playing area and back to the middle;
3. both teams run to the edge of the playing area and back to the middle;
4. all players fall to the ground as if fouled, scream in pain and then get back up on their feet quickly;
5. players turn to each other and give partner a High Five;
6. all players jump up and pretend to head a ball.

Introduce the instructions more gradually, depending on the age and experience of the players. (Warn players to be careful when returning to the middle, in order to prevent collisions).

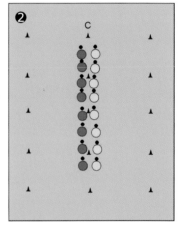

❷ Players then get a ball each and the coach gives the following instructions for players to follow:

1. the red team dribbles balls to the edge of the playing area and back to the middle;
2. the yellow team dribbles balls to the edge of the playing area and back to the middle;
3. both teams dribble balls to the edge of the playing area and back to the middle;
4. all players fall to the ground as if fouled, scream in pain then get back up on their feet quickly;
5. players pick up the balls, turn to each other and give their partner a High Five by hitting the balls against each other;
6. all players throw the balls in the air and jump up to catch them, bringing the balls into their chests like a goalkeeper.

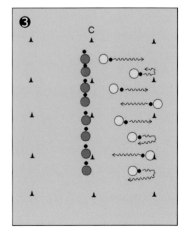

❸ Possible changes

- Make up some of your own instructions to follow, or add more to really get them thinking.
- Speed up the calls to add an extra challenge or, for example, call 'Four', whilst a team is dribbling, so they have to drop to the ground whilst on the move.

PIRATES AND BUCCANEERS

How it works

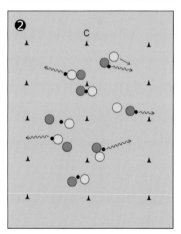

❶ Two teams stand opposite each other in pairs in the middle of a large playing area. Each player has the instep of their right foot resting against the ball, so it is trapped between their feet. On a signal from the coach, each partner tries to win possession of the ball by pushing against the ball with their foot. (Please ensure players have enough space at the start of this game, such as two or three metres between each pair).

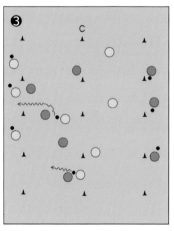

❷ Each player tries to get control of the ball and dribble it across to the opposite side of the playing area. There they must stop it, just past the sideline, (to get the treasure). Players can still win the ball back if their opponent has not reached the safety of the sideline.

❸ Play continues until one of each of all the pairs has crossed the sidelines. Players only score a point for their team if the ball is stopped, not if the ball is just kicked over the sideline with no control. (You can set up more cones at the sides to make a channel, within which the ball must be stopped). Repeat several times, changing from left to right feet in contact with the ball at the beginning of the game. Keep scores to make it more of a competition.

Possible changes

■ Change partners after two or four rounds.
■ Number each pair and the coach calls one number at a time, so that each pair competes one at a time.

SKITTLE BALL

How it works

❶ Two teams stand at each side of a rectangular play-ing area, with each player having a ball. A number of target cones are spaced out halfway between the two teams. On a signal from the coach, players try to pass their ball to hit one of the target cones in the centre of the playing area.

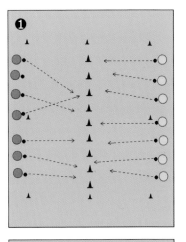

❷ On hitting a cone, the player runs into the middle and claims it for their team. Once the game has started, many balls will switch from one side to the other as players try to hit the target cones. Players may go into the playing area to get an unused ball, but they must bring it back to the edge of the playing area before passing at a target cone. In this diagram the score is level. A yellow player has just claimed a cone for their team, after the red team had already brought one back to their side of the playing area.

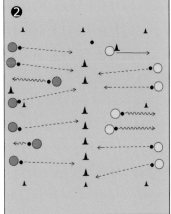

❸ This game has now finished as a yellow player has knocked over, and claimed, the last cone. The red team has won this round by five cones to four. Play several times and keep a running score.

Possible changes

■ If you're feeling brave, you can add one player from each team to act as a defender in the middle of the playing area. They can try to stop balls from the other team hitting the cones, and also pass balls back to their own team-mates.

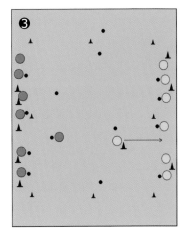

SKITTLE BALL 2

How it works

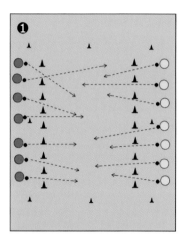

❶ Two teams stand at each side of a rectangular playing area, with each player having a ball. A number of target cones are spaced out on each side, just in front of both teams. On a signal from the coach, players try to pass their ball to hit one of the target cones at the opposite side of the playing area.

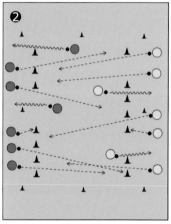

❷ Players must be very careful to either pass in between their own cones, or chip the ball over the top. If they accidentally knock over one of their own cones, then it stays down and counts as a hit. Once the game has started, many balls will switch from one side to the other as players try to hit the target cones. However, players may go into the playing area to get an unused ball, but they must bring it back to the edge of the playing area before passing at a target cone.

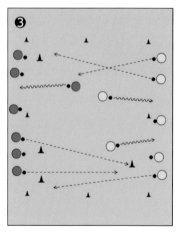

❸ This game has now finished as a red player has knocked over the last cone. Play several times and keep a running score, or play the best of three or five rounds.

Possible changes

■ Instead of playing until the last cone has been knocked over, play for a set amount of time and see which team has knocked over the most cones.

TARGET BALL

How it works

❶ Two teams stand at each side of a rectangular playing area, with each player having a ball. A number of target balls, (which must be a different colour to the balls used by the players), are spaced out halfway between the two teams. On a signal from the coach, players try to pass their ball to hit one of the target balls in the centre of the playing area.

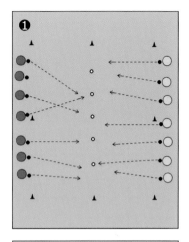

❷ Once the game has started, many balls will switch from one side to the other, as players try to hit the target balls. Players may go into the playing area to get an unused ball, but they must bring it back to the edge of the playing area before passing at a target ball. If a ball is knocked out of the side of the playing area, it can either be put back in by the coach, or left out until the next game.

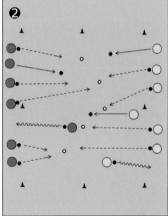

❸ Play for one to two minutes, and then score one point for a target ball in the other team's half of the playing area, and five points for a target ball that crosses the opposing team's side of the playing area. The game in the diagram has finished. The red team are awarded two points and the yellow team have seven points. Replace the target balls back in the middle and play again. Keep a running total to get a winning team after several rounds.

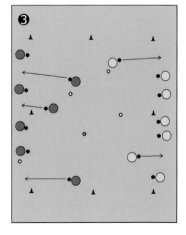

STAR WARS

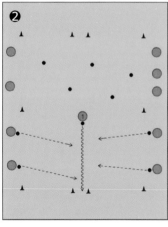

How it works

❶ Red Player One tries to dribble the ball, to get through the cone gate at the other end of the playing area. The other players try to pass their ball in order to hit the ball of Player One. (Stress hitting through the middle of the ball, to keep it down).

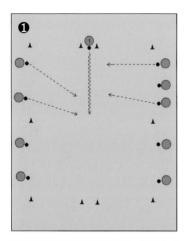

❷ If Player One's ball is hit, they go back to the side and another player goes to the end to attempt the challenge. If Player One gets to the other end, then give the other players fifteen seconds to reload their missiles, (get a ball ready), before the player sets off to try and get back. Player One then keeps going until their ball is hit. Set individual records which players could try and beat on another occasion.

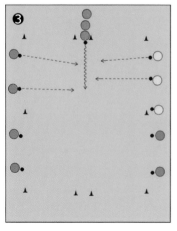

❸ Possible changes

■ You can play this as a team challenge, especially if you have a larger group, where each player gets one attempt to keep going until their ball is hit and they are knocked out. Combine the individual results, to get a team score that the others then have to try and beat.

■ Play a one versus one duel, by having each player starting at opposite ends. The player who lasts the longest, or gets the furthest, is the winner.

SWAMP MONSTERS

How it works

❶ Players are divided into three teams, as shown in the diagram, each player with a ball at their feet. The teams at each side become the Swamp Monsters and have to try and stop the other players from laying stepping stones, to cross the swamp safely. On a signal from the coach, all the red team dribble their balls through the cone gate.

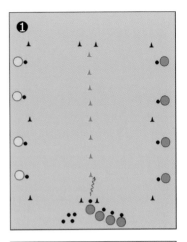

❷ Red players have to dribble a ball and stop it next to one of the red cones, (stepping stones), up the middle of the playing area. Players in the blue and yellow teams, (Swamp Monsters), have to try and knock the balls away from the middle cones. They are allowed to use a ball from the other team that has missed and gone across to the other side. They can also run into the middle to retrieve a ball, but can only pass it from the side to the playing area.

❸ When a ball has been knocked away from a middle cone, a red player has to dribble it back to the same cone and stop it there again. Now that nearly all the stepping stones are laid, the other red players are trying to stop any other balls being knocked away.

The game ends when the red team has every stepping stone, (ball next to a cone), in place. Swap teams and the next team have to try and beat the target time set by the red players.

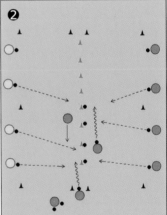

Possible changes

■ Set a two to three-minute time limit for each team; the winners are the team that has the most stepping stones in place during any part of that time period.

■ If a ball has been knocked away from a middle cone, the red player must dribble it through one of the end cones, before being allowed to replace it.

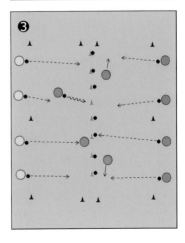

THREE CONE GAME

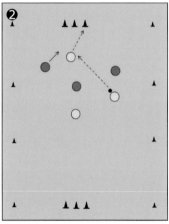

How it works

❶ Play three versus three, with normal game rules, but no players can use their hands. The yellow team try to dribble/pass the ball between them, to advance up the playing area.

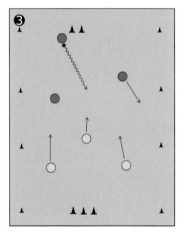

❷ Red players defend the cones at their end of the playing area. The yellow team can score by knocking down one of the cones. This cone must then stay down, so next time the yellow team tries to score, they only have two cones to aim at.

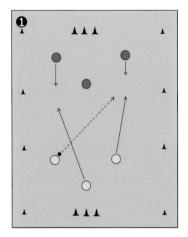

❸ The red team now gets possession of the ball, and the yellow team must retreat into their half to give the red players a chance to get going. The red team now tries to score against the yellow team by knocking down one of their cones.

Possible changes

■ You can play any numbers on each side, or have more cones to knock down.

■ A small, semi-circular, cone exclusion area, can be set up around the cone goals if players persist in standing right in front of the cone(s) when defending.

GOALIE WENT

How it works

❶ When we used to play soccer at school we had a rule called 'Goalie Went'. This meant that the goalkeeper was allowed to leave the box, and then any other player could become the goalkeeper if they happened to be nearest the goal at that time.

   This rule applies in this game, which is played with three versus three players under normal game rules, apart from 'Goalie Went'. The yellow team starts with possession and they have to try and dribble/pass the ball between them to advance up the field of play.

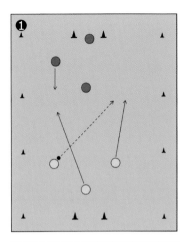

❷ The red team defend the goal at their end of the playing area. One of the red players must stay in the goal as long as the yellow team have possession. Yellow players continue to attack as they have possession of the ball.

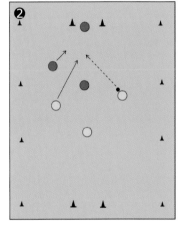

❸ As soon as the yellow team lose possession, one of their players must drop back into the goal, giving the red team a three versus two advantage in the middle of the field. If the red team score a goal, then they return to two players and a goalkeeper, and the yellow team start with possession at their own goal.

Possible changes

■ You can play this game with any number on each side.

■ To give the team in possession even more of an advantage, one player has to drop back into the goal, and another player has to leave the field of play until a goal is scored, or possession is won back by their team.

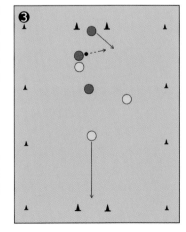

MUSICAL CONES

How it works

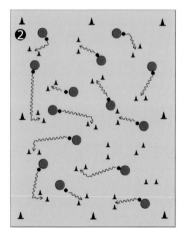

❶ Players have a ball each and dribble around the playing area, keeping control of the ball. There must be more small cones spread around the area than there are players.

❷ On a signal from the coach, players must dribble their ball to a cone inside the playing area, stop the ball under their foot and pick up a cone to place on top of their head.

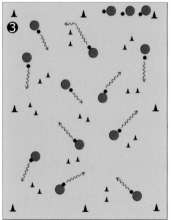

❸ Play a few rounds and then start to remove a cone each time, until there is at least one less cone than there are players. At this point the last player left without a cone is out.

Continue removing cones until you are left with a winner. If players try to stay dribbling around a cone then they can be warned at first, but then removed from the game if necessary. If you have a portable CD player then it makes the game a lot more fun, with players dribbling for the cones when the music stops.

CONE GATES DRIBBLING

How it works

❶ All the players have a ball each and dribble it around, keeping control of it inside the playing area. There are the same number of cone gates as players. Players are not allowed to dribble through the gates.

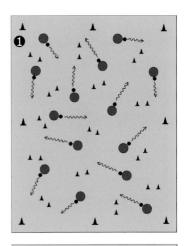

❷ On a given signal, (either a number, or the name of the skill), from the coach, all the players have to dribble their ball to an empty cone gate and perform one of the following skills:

- ◼ alternate instep foot touches;
- ◼ toe taps on top of the ball;
- ◼ figure of eight dribble around the cones;
- ◼ sit on the ball;
- ◼ stationary step-overs.

Add any more in that you can think of, but you may need to demonstrate each of these in turn and add them in gradually.

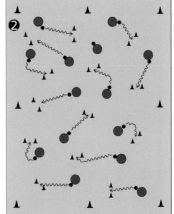

❸ **Possible changes**
- ◼ Challenge players to dribble through as many different cone gates as they can in thirty seconds, or one minute. They must go through a different cone gate each time. Can they go through them all within the time limit? If they do it again, can they beat their last score?
- ◼ Pass the ball through the cones and run round the outside of the gate to collect the ball at the other side.

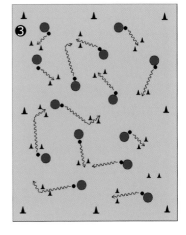

GUARDIANS OF THE CONES

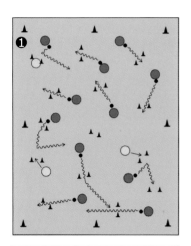

How it works

❶ The three yellow players need to wear a bib/pinny and be Guardians of the Cones. They do not tackle, but just move around stopping players getting through the cone gates, making them turn away to go through another. The red players must try to dribble through as many cone gates as possible in thirty seconds or one minute.

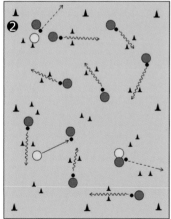

❷ **Possible changes**
■ Allow the Guardians of the Cones to tackle and kick the players' balls out of the area.

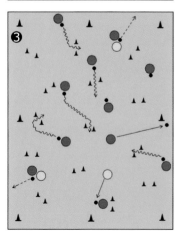

❸ Balls that are kicked out of the playing area can be retrieved, and the players can then continue dribbling through the cone gates.

■ How many cones can the red players dribble through altogether in one minute? (You will have to trust them to give a correct score as you add them up).
■ Choose three different Guardians of the Cones and see if they can stop the red players beating the previous total.

CONE GATES PASSING

How it works

❶ Players are in pairs and spread out around the edge of the playing area with a ball between them. The first player runs into the playing area and must go through a cone gate, before running back to their partner. The second player must then run through a different cone gate, before going back to their partner. Players must continue to go through a different cone gate each time. How many different cone gates can the pairs go through in thirty seconds or one minute?

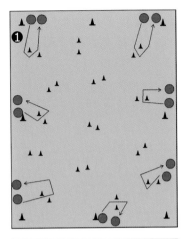

❷ This time the first player dribbles into the playing area and must go through a cone gate before passing back to their partner. The second player must then dribble through a different cone gate before passing back to their partner. Players must continue to go through a different cone gate each time. As they travel further away, they may want to dribble the ball part of the way back and then pass. How many different cone gates can the pairs go through in thirty seconds or one minute?

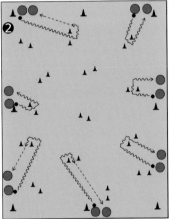

❸ Red players now start either side of a cone gate. Partners must make five passes, before they move to a different cone gate and do the same again. Reduce the number of passes to three and repeat. Then they must pass the ball through the cone gate only once before moving on. How many cone gates can they do in thirty seconds or one minute?

Possible changes
■ One touch passes through the cone gate.

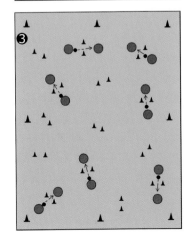

GUARDIANS OF THE CONES 2

How it works

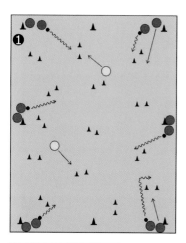

❶ Players begin in pairs around the side of the playing area, with a ball between them. Get two of the players to wear a bib/pinny and be Guardians of the Cones. On a signal from the coach, the pairs enter the playing area.

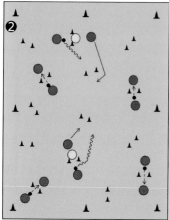

❷ Red players just try to make one pass before moving to a different cone gate. The Guardians of the Cones do not tackle, but just move around stopping players getting through a gate, by standing between the cones, making them turn away to go through another gate.

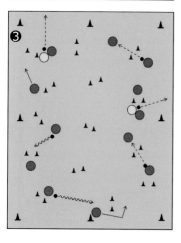

❸ Possible changes

- Allow the Guardians of the Cones to tackle and kick the balls out of the area. Balls that are kicked out of the playing area can be retrieved and partners can continue to pass through the cone gates, or that pair can be eliminated from the game.
- How many cones can the red partners pass through altogether in thirty seconds or one minute? (You will have to trust them to give a correct score as you add them up).
- Choose two different Guardians of the Cones and see if they can stop the red players beating the previous total.

CONE GATE TAG

How it works

❶ The yellow players stand at one end of the grid and must try and get to the other end without being tagged. All the yellow players can go at the same time, or you can send them in two separate groups.

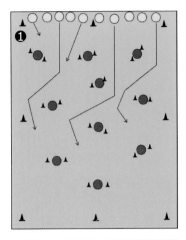

❷ The red players stand in the cone gates. They must keep at least one foot between the cones at all times, but can step out with the other foot and reach to tag players as they pass. If a player is tagged they must go back to the start and try again. Swap the teams over after a few turns.

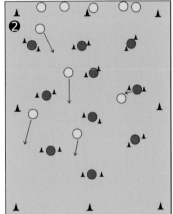

❸ Repeat with each of the players dribbling a ball.

Possible changes

■ Any player tagged gets two cones, and makes another cone gate inside the playing area, making it gradually more and more difficult to get through. Can any players become the Cone Gate Tag Champions?

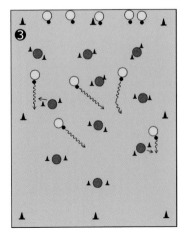

THROUGH THE GATE

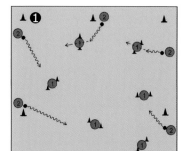

How it works

❶ Half the players stand in a cone gate, whilst the other half stand around the outside of the playing area with a ball at their feet. On the first signal from the coach, Player Twos start dribbling the ball inside the playing area. They have to try and pass the ball through the legs of as many Player Ones as they can in one minute. Can they get round them all in that time? Change roles and Player Ones try to beat the best time, or the greatest number of passes through the legs by any one player.

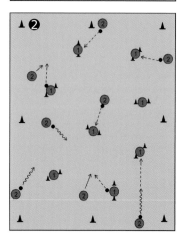

❷ This time Player Twos enter the playing area and must pass the ball to any Player One. Player One passes the ball back to them, and they then dribble the ball towards another Player One to repeat this one-two passing sequence. Can they get round them all within one or two minutes? Change roles and Player Ones try to beat the best time, or the greatest number of passes.

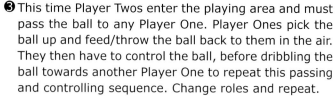

❸ This time Player Twos enter the playing area and must pass the ball to any Player One. Player Ones pick the ball up and feed/throw the ball back to them in the air. They then have to control the ball, before dribbling the ball towards another Player One to repeat this passing and controlling sequence. Change roles and repeat.

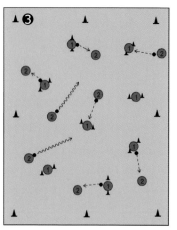

Possible changes

- Players could request the type of feed or throw, such as knee, chest etc., to make it easier.
- Player Ones in the cone gates start with a ball. Player Twos run into the playing area, call for the ball, receive a pass and then pass it back, before moving on to repeat this passing sequence with a different Player One. This could be repeated but receiving a feed/or throw to head the ball back to Player Ones.

LOCKED IN THE STOCKS

How it works

❶ The yellow players, (wearing bibs/pinnies), chase after the red players, who run away but must stay in the playing area. If tagged, the red player must be taken to one of the cone gates and locked in the stocks, with their feet spread apart next to each of the cones.

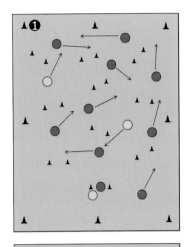

❷ These players can only be freed from the stocks if another red player crawls through their legs. Play for one or two minutes, or until all the red players are 'locked in the stocks'. Swap the chasers and play again if you wish. The new group must try to beat the number of red players locked in the stocks after one or two minutes, or get all the red players locked away in a quicker time.

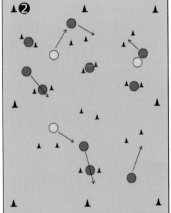

❸ This time each of the red players has a ball and tries to avoid being tagged by one of the yellow players, who still don't have a ball. If tagged, the red player must be taken to the stocks and stand still with their feet apart, holding the ball above their head. Red players can only be freed if another player passes the ball through their legs.

You will notice that there are only two yellow chasers this time, as it is easier for them to tag the red players. Swap the chasers and play again if you wish. The new group have to try to beat the number of red players locked away after one or two minutes, or get all red players 'locked in the stocks' in a quicker time.

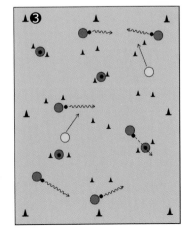

HALF AND HALF

How it works

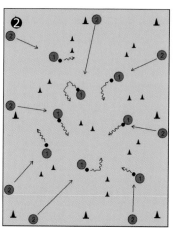

❶ Half the players stand in a cone gate with a ball at their feet, whilst the other half stand around the outside of the playing area without a ball. On the first signal from the coach, Player Ones with a ball start dribbling around inside the playing area.

❷ On a second signal from the coach, Player Twos can enter the playing area and attempt to win possession of a ball by tackling any other red player. There must only be two players in any tackle at any time. If a ball is lost outside the playing area, the coach could pass it back in to any player without a ball, or nominate a player without a ball to retrieve it.

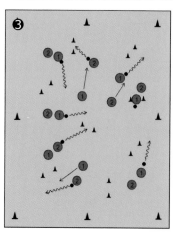

❸ Any red player can dribble a ball and stop it between the cones of a gate. That player is then safe for five seconds, but after that they must leave the gate in any direction. Play for one or two minutes and all the players in possession of a ball gain a point. Play again with all those not in possession, starting the next game with a ball. Who has the most points at the end of several rounds?

Possible changes

■ Play as a team game and see how many balls Player Ones are in possession of at the end, compared to Player Twos.

ONE VERSUS ALL

How it works

❶ All the red players stand in a cone gate with a ball at their feet. A yellow player stands at the end of the playing area without a ball. On a signal from the coach, the yellow player can enter the playing area and try to win a ball from any of the red players.

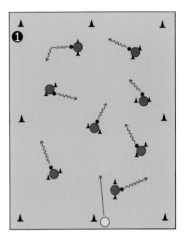

❷ If the yellow player wins a ball and kicks it out of the playing area, the red player must then go and stand back in a cone gate. Any red player can dribble a ball and stop it between the cones of a gate. That player is then safe for five seconds, but after that they must leave the gate in any direction.

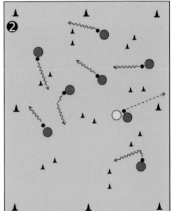

❸ Play for a set time limit of two or three minutes, and then change the yellow player to see if they can complete the challenge, or set a new One versus All record.

Possible changes

■ Allow the red players who still have a ball to pass to the other red players, standing in a cone gate to help keep possession. The ball must be passed back within a five-second time limit.

■ Start with two yellow players if you have a larger group, or want to make it more difficult for the red players.

■ If a yellow player can win a ball, dribble it to a cone gate and stop it under control, then the red player from whom they won possession of the ball becomes another yellow player. That gate cannot then be used as a safe place for any of the other red players.

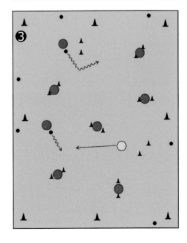

CONE GATES POSSESSION

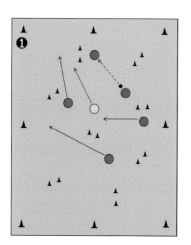

How it works
❶ Five red players try and keep possession of the ball within the playing area. The red team gets one point for every completed pass.

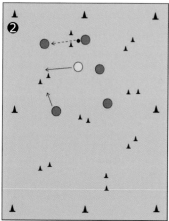

❷ The red team receive five points if they can complete a pass through a cone gate. They cannot pass through the same gate twice in succession.

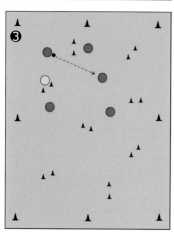

❸ The yellow player tries to prevent passes through the cone gates, (as in the diagram), and, if possible, wins the ball and kicks it out of the playing area. Play for one or two minutes, or until the yellow player has won possession and kicked the ball out of the playing area three times, whichever comes first. Change the yellow player with one of the red players and try to beat the previous best point score.

Possible changes
■ Play with six versus two, five versus three, or even four versus four, depending on the age and ability of the group.

CONE GATES POSSESSION 2

How it works

❶ A red player stands at one end of the playing area with a ball at their feet. A yellow player stands at the other end of the playing area without a ball. On a signal from the coach, both players can enter the playing area. The red player must dribble and pass the ball through the legs of another red player standing in a cone gate.

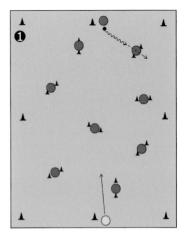

❷ That player then becomes free and can dribble to pass through the legs of another player, or pass the ball back to the player who freed them. The red team then has to try and keep possession of the ball within the playing area, whilst freeing as many other players as possible.

   If the yellow player intercepts or tackles the ball and kicks it out of the playing area, then they become a red player for the next game, and the person who made the mistake becomes the yellow defender. Change the starting red player and have the others start in different gates. Can they free all their team without losing possession and within a two-minute time limit?

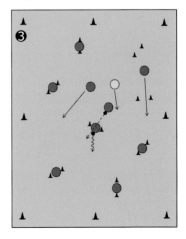

❸ **Possible changes**
   ■ Have one of the red players standing in a gate, start the game holding a ball. When this player is freed, the red team then have to keep possession of both balls from the yellow defender.
   ■ Start with two red players at one end, with a ball each and two yellow defenders.

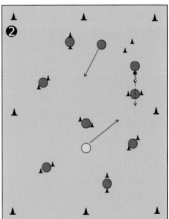

CONE GATES GAME

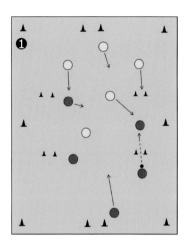

How it works

❶ Play five versus five under normal game rules, but no goalkeepers are allowed. If any team completes a pass, or dribbles the ball through a cone gate in their own half of the playing area, they get one point.

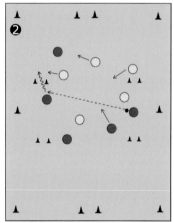

❷ If any team completes a pass, or dribbles the ball through a cone gate in the other team's half of the playing area, they get two points.

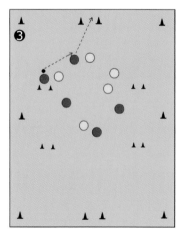

❸ If they score a goal they get three points. If the yellow team win possession then they attempt to do the same, scoring as many points as possible. Can either team achieve a 'perfect goal' by going through a gate in each half of the playing area and then scoring, which would equal six points altogether.

Possible changes

■ A team must complete one or two passes through a cone gate before they are allowed to score a goal.

CHAPTER 2

Large Area Drills – Intermediate

Continuing on the same journey, this next collection of drills uses the same playing area, but the organization is perhaps more complex and a wider range of skills are required. The emphasis is still on having fun and maximum participation, but the players are required to develop much more of, what I call, a 'soccer brain'. It is one thing to be athletic or develop good technique, but without this sense of awareness or intelligence about the game, a player will be limited in their ability to function well as part of a team. Instinctively knowing how to react to the myriad different situations you may find yourself in, within a game of soccer, is a difficult thing to achieve. But to promote this intuition, coaches need to be inventive and create sessions that stimulate such thought processes, offering a variety of challenges to which the players have to respond.

With this in mind, don't forget to check out the 'possible changes' section at the end of many of these drills. Here you will find suggestions as to how the drill can be adapted to suit a younger audience, or how it can be extended for individuals, or the whole group. It is up to you, as the coach, to create the right environment, whereby your players will enjoy and thrive on this sense of challenge, whilst making the most of each and every player's unique talents.

POSSIBLE SESSIONS

The following selections are only suggestions as to how drills could be combined to create a one, or two-hour session. As a teacher, or coach you need to assess the ability of your group and take into account possible numbers, before making appropriate choices of your own. All these sessions could also be started with a warm-up of your own, and ended with some regular, small-sided games.

- Goldmine
- Hungry Hippos
- Prison Break

- Inside Out
- Knockout Whist Ball
- Possession Challenge
- End to End
- Quick Change

- Passing by Numbers
- Rollerball
- Possession Challenge 3

- Ball Raiders 2
- Through the Middle

- Coach in the Middle

- Invader
- Score in the Middle

GOLDMINE

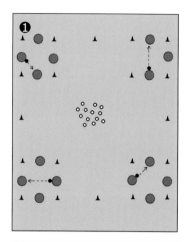

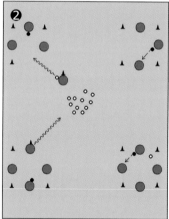

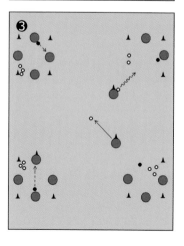

How it works

❶ Teams of three or four start inside each grid, at the corners of the playing area. Place a large number of balls in the middle of the playing area; each of these represents a gold nugget, buried deep in the mine. Players work together in each grid, passing the ball to each other.

❷ When a team has completed ten passes, one of them has to put on a mining helmet, (cone), and run into the mine to get a golden nugget, (ball). They then dribble the ball back to their square and start again to complete another ten passes. In this diagram the teams have progressed as follows:

- **Top left:** the team has completed ten passes and a player is on the way back from the mine with a gold nugget.
- **Top right:** the team still have to complete their ten passes, before going to the mine.
- **Bottom left:** the team has completed ten passes and a player has just put on their mining helmet to go into the mine.
- **Bottom right:** the team has already got a gold nugget and has started on their next set of ten passes.

❸ In this diagram the game is nearly over. Each team has collected three gold nuggets from the mine. (A different player must put on the helmet and go into the mine each time). The team in the bottom right is just about to win, as a player is running out to collect the last gold nugget. Put the balls back in the middle and play again. Keep a running total of the number of gold nuggets collected by each team.

Possible changes

Depending on the age and ability of the group, the skill performed in the grid can be changed to any of the following:

- pass and move combinations, (for example, Round the Cone drill).
- headers, side-foot or laces volleys, out of their own hands, or fed by another player.

BALL THIEF

How it works
❶ Teams of two or three players start outside each grid at the corners of the playing area. On a signal from the coach, the first player from each team runs into the middle of the playing area.

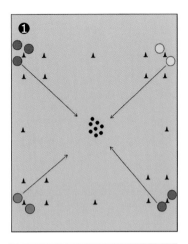

❷ Players must then dribble a ball back to the team's square. The ball must be stopped inside the square, before the next player in the team can go and do the same.

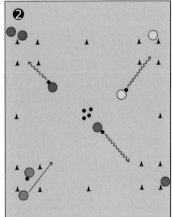

❸ In this diagram, the bottom right team are just about to get the last ball from the middle of the playing area. When this happens, players are allowed to become a ball thief and steal one from another team's square. The first team to get three balls inside their square is the winner. Put the balls back in the middle and play again.

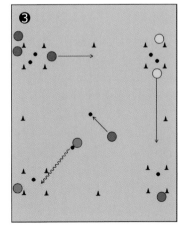

Possible changes
■ Start with a lot of balls and then take one out of the middle after each game to make it gradually more and more difficult.

■ One player from each team can play the whole game, rather than doing a relay. You could have a competition with knock-out rounds and semi-finals/finals to get a Ball Thief Champion. (This can be very tiring, so allow recovery team between rounds).

ULTIMATE BALL THIEF

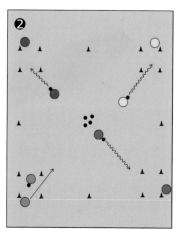

How it works

❶ Teams of two or three players start outside each grid, at the corners of the playing area. On a signal from the coach, the first player from each team runs into the middle of the playing area.

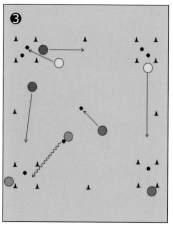

❷ Players must then dribble a ball back to their own team's square. The ball must be stopped inside the square before the next player in the team can go and do the same.

❸ Once the first, (or second), ball has been stopped in the square, any player on any team is then allowed to steal a ball from another team's square. You can allow players to only steal a ball from a square, or you can let them tackle others to win a ball anywhere inside the playing area. The first team to get three balls stopped inside their square is the winner. Equal teams are needed for this one, and a second pair of eyes is often handy as a lot of cheating can go on – but you'll have great fun!

HUNGRY HIPPOS

How it works

❶ If you've played the children's game of the same name, then you will have an idea of how this drill works. The red players dribble their ball anywhere inside the playing area, except for the small grids in each corner. On a signal from the coach, the yellow players, (Hungry Hippos), run into the playing area to try and win a ball from any one of the red players.

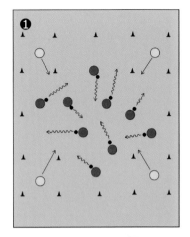

❷ Here we can see that two yellow players, (Hungry Hippos), have won a ball and are dribbling it back to stop it inside their grid. As soon as they have done this, they are allowed to turn and run back into the centre to try and win another ball. The other two yellow players are still attempting to tackle and win a ball from a red player. The red players are allowed to try and win their ball back, until it has been dribbled inside a corner grid.

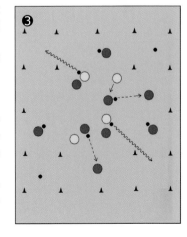

❸ If a player loses control of a ball and it goes outside the playing area, then it is lost and cannot be retrieved. A red player who has lost their ball can still help others by being available for a pass when a Hungry Hippo challenges a team-mate. The game continues until all the balls have been won by a yellow player, or lost out of the playing area. The Hippo who gets the least number of balls inside their grid is knocked out and becomes another red player, with a ball in the middle. The game then restarts with just three Hungry Hippos and so on, until you have a winner.

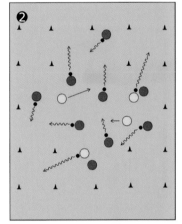

Possible changes

■ The Hippos work as a team to try and win as many balls as they can, within a certain time limit. A new group then become the Hippos to try and beat the previous score.

■ Play it as a tagging game, with the tagged red players being taken to stand inside the grid of the catching Hippo.

ATTACK OF THE GREEN GOBLINS

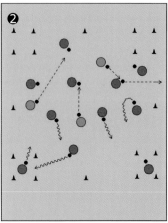

How it works

❶ Each of the red players has a ball and is a Spiderman. They must keep control of their ball inside the playing area. The squares in each corner are safe zones for any Spiderman to dribble into, if in trouble. However, if another Spiderman enters the safe zone, the other must leave. The green players are the Green Goblins and they also have a ball.

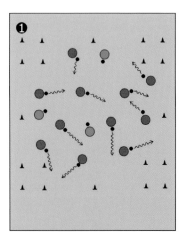

❷ The Green Goblins must try to pass their ball to hit the ball of one of the Spidermen. If a red player's ball is hit, they are out of the game and must stand outside the playing area. As more players are knocked out, the coach can reduce the number of safe zones by removing the inside cone of the square.

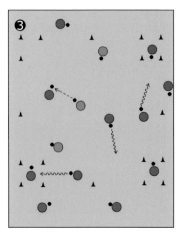

❸ In this diagram, the Green Goblins have hit the balls of four Spidermen and they are standing outside the playing area. The coach has removed the inside cone of the top left safety zone, as several players are out of the game. They will remove another if one more player is knocked out. Swap different players into the roles of the Green Goblins and play again.

Possible changes

■ Play as a straightforward tag game with no balls.
■ Play that a Spiderman turns into another Green Goblin when hit, but they will need to put on a green bib/pinny.

PRISON BREAK

How it works

❶ Two teams play a six versus six game. Two members of each team, however, are stuck in prison, (cone square), at the opposite end of the playing area.

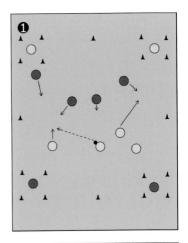

❷ The blue team in possession of the ball, must try to pass it to one of their team stuck in prison. The player in prison must control and stop the ball, within the corner grid, to be set free. They are then replaced by a different player from the same team.

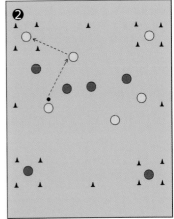

❸ The red team then restart play with a pass from that end of the playing area. The game continues until one of the teams wins, by freeing every one of their players from prison. No player goes into prison twice, so when five players have been set free, that team will have a five versus four advantage in the game, but the other team may find it easier to defend only one prison.

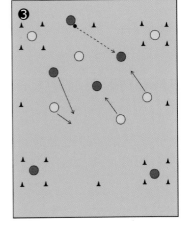

Possible changes

■ Alter the size of the corner squares, depending on the ability of the players.

■ Just play to free the two players who are in prison at the start of the game, and then begin a new game with two different players in prison.

SAFETY ZONE

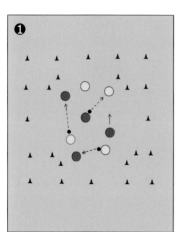

How it works

❶ Four players of each team move around the central area passing the ball. Red players can only pass to yellow players, and they must pass back to a red player.

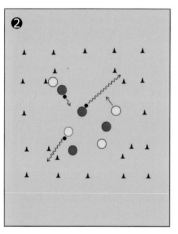

❷ On a signal from the coach, players in possession must try to dribble the ball through a gate, to stop it in one of the four safety zones. Players can attempt to tackle opponents to gain possession. If they win possession, they can then attempt to dribble the ball into a safety zone. If a ball goes out of the playing area, then it is lost for that round.

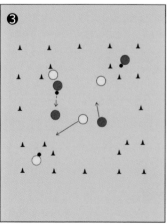

❸ Players are allowed to pass to a team-mate, who is better placed to dribble the ball into a safety zone. The game in this diagram has ended up being three versus three, with the red team trying to get the only ball left through a cone gate. The yellow team are trying to defend the entrances to the safety zones, and also trying to intercept or tackle for the ball.

Possible changes

■ Play the game five versus five, using four balls or six versus six, using five balls, and so on, but adjust the size of the playing area accordingly.

■ Play for two or three rounds and then remove one of the safety zones, and so on, until the last round has only one left.

FOUR CORNER POSSESSION

How it works

❶ The four red players in each corner square must stay within that area. The two yellow and red players in the central playing area can go anywhere, except inside each of the corner squares. The red players have to try and keep possession from the yellow defenders.

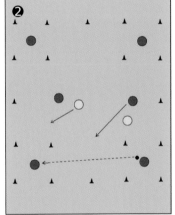

❷ The red team can pass between themselves in any way that they like, from corner to corner, (as in the diagram), or back into the central area. If a red player loses control of the ball outside of the playing area, then the red team has to start their pass count again. Challenge the players to keep possession for a set amount of time, or number of passes. After several minutes, change roles and then try and beat the previous record.

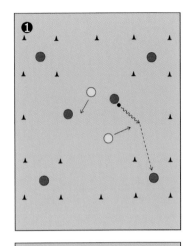

❸ Possible changes

- If the yellow players intercept the ball and can pass it to a player in a corner square, then they change roles with the red players in the centre. To make it easier, play with two or three versus one players inside the central area, or add more yellow players to make it more difficult for the team in possession.
- Players in the corner grids must pass to a player in the central area, or restrict the red players to two touches on the ball.
- The corner players are allowed into the central area after receiving a pass, (as in the diagram). Can the red team free all four corner players without losing possession?

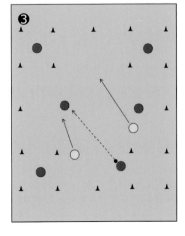

CORNER BALL

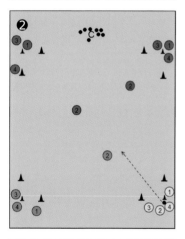

How it works

❶ Four different teams stand behind a large cone goal, at each corner of the playing area. The coach has a large supply of balls and passes/throws a ball into the middle, calling a number as they do so. That number player from each team enters the playing area and can compete for the ball, or stay back to defend their goal. In this diagram, Blue Player Two has got possession of the ball and has dribbled past Yellow Player Two and scored a goal.

❷ Player Twos from the red and green teams have decided to hold back and defend their goal. Yellow Player Two is now out of the game, but the other players stay in. Yellow Player Four passes/throws the ball back into the playing area, and the three remaining players compete for the ball or defend their goal. Now Green Player Two has got to the ball first, so must try and score in the red or blue goal. If the ball is kicked out of the playing area the coach passes/throws in another ball quickly for the game to continue.

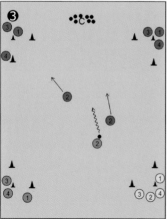

❸ Allow two minutes maximum for each game. Score as follows if a player has not won outright when the time is up:

- Player scores in every goal = four points;
- Two players still in the game = three points each;
- Three players still in the game = two points each;
- Four players still in the game = one point each.

The coach then calls another number and the game starts again.

Possible changes

- If you're brave you could call out two numbers at the same time but I prefer to keep it to one from each team at a time.

CORNER BALL 2

How it works

❶ Four different teams stand behind a large corner goal. The coach has a large supply of balls and passes/throws a ball into the middle, towards the orange player. As the coach passes the ball into play they shout two colours, for example red and yellow.

The first of those two colours becomes the defended goal by Red Player One, joined by the player from the second colour called out, in this case Yellow Player One. Blue and Green Player Ones join sides with the orange player in possession of the ball, to try and score in the red goal.

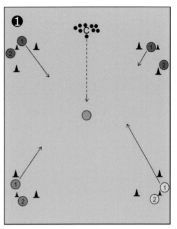

❷ Red Player One has held back to act as a goalkeeper whilst Yellow Player One has tried to close down the orange player as quickly as possible. The orange player, coming under pressure, has passed the ball to Blue Player One.

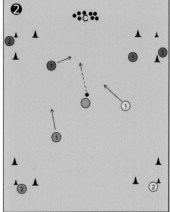

❸ In this example, Blue Player One has been able to take a quick shot at goal. If the blue player scores, then each player from the attacking teams gain a point. All players then go back behind their goals and the game is repeated with Player Twos. If the red or yellow players gain possession of the ball, then they attempt to score in either of the blue or green goals. If they do so, then each player from the defending team gains two points. If the ball goes out of play, the game can either be finished, or restarted with a throw-in from the edge of the area. Play several rounds and then count up the points to find the winning colour team.

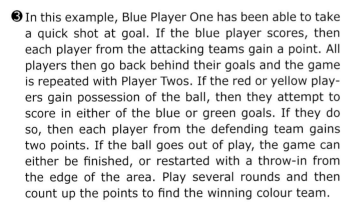
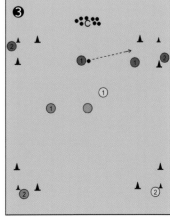

Possible changes

■ Have both players of each colour come in at the same time, to make it a five versus four game.

SURPRISE ATTACK

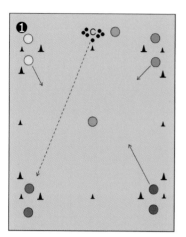

How it works

❶ The coach calls out a colour and that player becomes the defender, being joined by the orange player in the centre of the square to defend that goal. At the same time, the coach passes a ball into any of the other three players and all of them become attackers, to make a three versus two game.

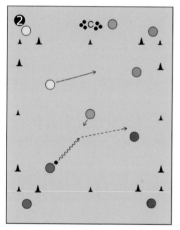

❷ In this diagram the coach has called green, and passed the ball to the blue player. The orange and green players now have to defend that goal.

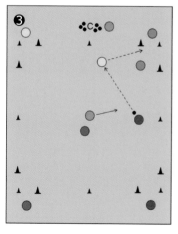

❸ The blue, red and yellow players have to try and keep possession, by passing or dribbling to create a scoring opportunity, but need to remember which goal they are attacking! If the defending players win possession of the ball, they can win the game by scoring in any of the other three goals. If the ball is kicked out of play, the coach can pass/throw in another ball to continue the game, or call time. When the game is over, the other players come into the goals and those who have just played stand out of the playing area. Swap the orange defenders after a few games.

Possible changes

■ Have all the players come into the playing area to make it six versus four.

FOUR GOAL SHOOTOUT

How it works

❶ This is a four-goal game, with a goalkeeper in each goal and three versus one players in the middle of the playing area, the size of which will depend on the age of the players. A goalkeeper starts the game by passing a ball to one of the attacking red players.

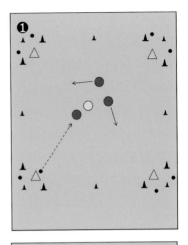

❷ Attacking players try to combine to create scoring opportunities. The red team must attempt to score in a different goal to the one that the first pass came from.

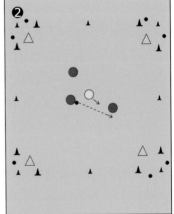

❸ Play then restarts from the goal into which a shot was taken. Have some balls ready, close to the goals, to keep the play moving if a shot is missed. Change goalkeepers for other players after a few rounds.

Possible changes

■ Play three versus two players in the middle, to make it harder for the attacking team.

■ The red players can only have two touches on the ball.

■ The coach numbers the goals one to four, and calls the number of the goal that the red team must try to score in.

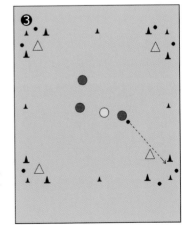

INSIDE OUT

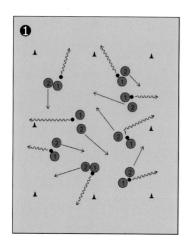

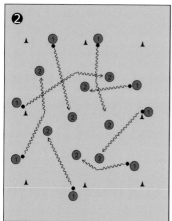

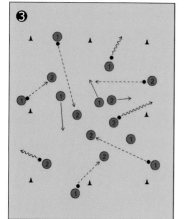

How it works
❶ Players stand in pairs within a large playing area. On a signal from the coach, Player Ones jog to the outside of the playing area, whilst Player Twos jog around the inside of the playing area. When Player Ones get outside the playing area they must turn, look for their partner and jog/run/sprint back to them to tag them. Player Twos then repeat this by jogging to the outside, whilst Player Ones jog around the inside. After one or two minutes, Player Ones then get a ball at their feet. On a signal from the coach, Player Ones dribble the ball to the outside of the playing area, whilst Player Twos jog around the inside.

❷ When Player Ones get outside the playing area they must turn, look for their partner, dribble the ball to them and stop it at their feet. Player Twos then repeat this by dribbling the ball to the outside, whilst Player Ones jog around the inside.

❸ After one or two minutes, repeat the drill but this time the player who dribbles to the outside, must pass the ball back in to their partner, who must find space to receive inside the playing area.

Possible changes
- Make players run/dribble around one of the outside cones, before dribbling or passing back inside. Or make them perform a certain skill once outside the playing area, such as a drag back turn, before dribbling or passing back inside.
- The coach, or a pair of players, act as passive defenders, to make it more difficult for partners to find space inside the playing area to receive a pass.
- The player who dribbles to the outside, picks the ball up and throws it in for their partner to control before dribbling.

DOUBLE TROUBLE

How it works

❶ Players space out in a large coned area, with one yellow tagger for about every five or six runners. The yellow players try to tag the red players as quickly as possible.

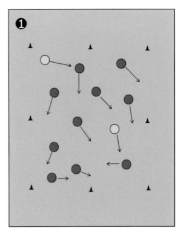

❷ The first red player tagged must go to the outside of the grid. When another red player is tagged, they can go to the outside of the grid and link hands with the other red player.

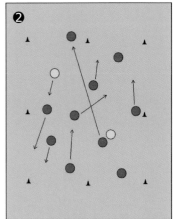

❸ This pair can then come back into the grid, and are allowed to shield other red players who have not yet been caught. Encourage the group to work together, to prevent the taggers from catching all the red players for as long as possible. Also, encourage the yellow taggers to work together, especially as more pairs come into the grid causing them 'double trouble'. Continue until all the players are tagged. The last players to be caught could start another game by being the new taggers.

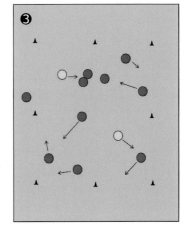

Possible changes

■ Allow free players to join a pair by linking hands at one end. When this happens, the player at the other side of the original pair is set free to run away from the taggers.

■ Play again, but this time red players have the ball.

PASSING BY NUMBERS

How it works

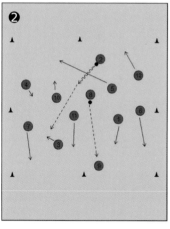

❶ All the players are given a number and they move around within the coned area.

The number of balls used will depend on how many are in the group. Player One must pass to Player Two and Player Seven must pass to Player Eight.

❷ Passes continue in sequence, with players making space to pass and receive.

❸ Player Twelve passes to Player One when they receive the ball.

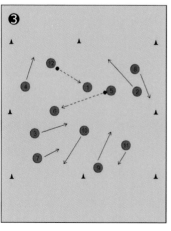

Possible changes
- Start by throwing the ball to get players moving.
- Add in an extra ball and/or a defender.
- Perform a turn or particular skill when receiving the ball.
- Even numbers pick up the ball, once controlled, and throw the ball in the air for odd numbers to control.
- If you have a large number of players, then run the same practise in two grids. Odd or even numbers can then move into the other grid, after making their pass.

ROLLERBALL

How it works
❶ Red players must dribble their ball inside the playing area. On a signal from the coach, the yellow players must roll their ball, to try and hit the ball of a red player.

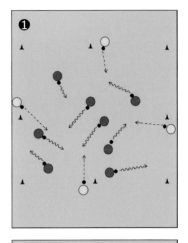

❷ Hit or miss, yellow players have to retrieve their ball and get back to the side of the playing area, before they can roll it in again. Red players are allowed to pass a ball to each other to try and prevent it from being hit.

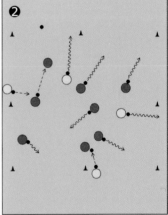

❸ Only two players are now left with a ball, but they continue to help each other by passing quickly between each other, to make the balls difficult to hit. Play continues until there is only one ball left, and then a count begins to see how many passes the red players can make before the last ball is hit. Change the yellow players on the outside and play again to try and beat the previous overall time, or pass count on the last ball.

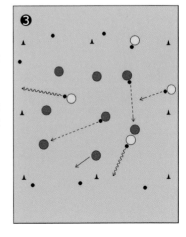

Possible changes
■ When a red player's ball is hit, they are out of the game and stand outside the playing area until the next round.

POSSESSION CHALLENGE

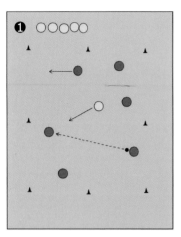

How it works

❶ Divide the group into two equal teams. The red team tries to keep possession of the ball for a set number of passes, (five to ten), or a set amount of time, (twenty to thirty seconds).

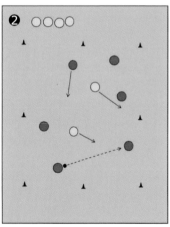

❷ If they succeed, a second player from the yellow team enters the playing area.

   The pass, or time count, starts again to try and keep possession.

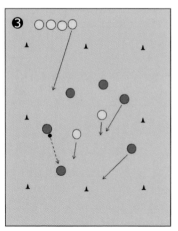

❸ If the set number of passes is completed, then another yellow player enters the playing area and so on. If the yellow players intercept the ball (they must have control of the ball in order for it to count), or the red team lose control of the ball outside the playing area, then the teams swap roles. Teams compete against each other to keep possession of the ball for the greatest number of passes, or amount of time. Swap the order that the defending players enter the playing area, each time they play.

Possible changes

■ Allow three errors before the teams swap over. After each error, continue the pass count from where the mistake occurred.

POSSESSION CHALLENGE 2

How it works

❶ Red players outnumber the yellow player by around eight to one. The red team tries to keep possession of the ball for a set amount of time, (twenty to thirty seconds), or for a set number of passes, (five to ten).

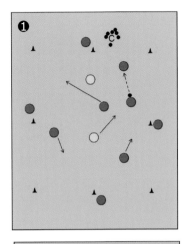

❷ When the set amount of time, or the target number of passes is completed, the coach plays another ball into the playing area for the red team to keep in possession.

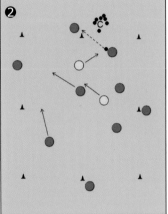

❸ This continues until all the red players have possession of a ball, or until the yellow player knocks a ball out of the playing area. The yellow player then swaps with a red player and the game can begin again with one ball. Challenge the group to better the number of balls in play, before the new yellow player can gain possession of a ball and kick it out of the playing area.

Possible changes

■ Include another defender to make it eight versus two.

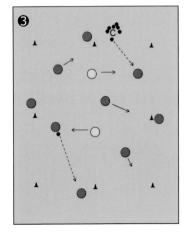

POSSESSION CHALLENGE 3

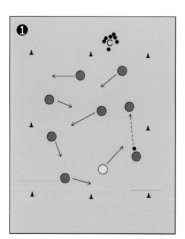

How it works

❶ Play five versus two inside the playing area, but with four extra red players outside. The red team tries to keep possession of the ball for a set number of passes, (five to ten), or amount of time, (ten to twenty seconds).

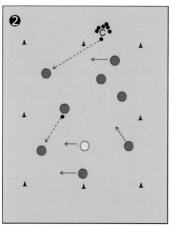

❷ The red players on the outside can move along the edge of playing area to receive and pass the ball to other red players.

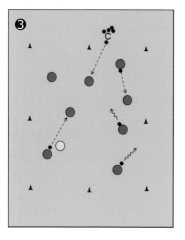

❸ When the set number of passes is completed, the coach plays another ball into the playing area for the red team to keep in possession. This continues until all the red players within the playing area have posses-sion of a ball, or until the yellow players knock a ball out of the playing area. The players then swap roles and the game can begin again with one ball.

Possible changes

■ Include another defender to make it four versus three players inside the playing area.

■ You can also just have two or three players around the outside.

DROP OUT

How it works

❶ There are two teams of around six players. The six red players try to keep possession of the ball from just three of the yellow players, who are allowed inside the playing area.

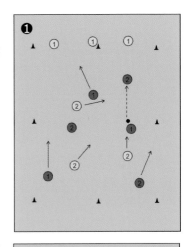

❷ As soon as the yellow players win possession, the rest of the yellow team needs to enter the playing area and support their team-mates as quickly as possible. The three Red Player Ones must drop out to their end of the playing area. The yellow team then tries to keep possession for as long as possible.

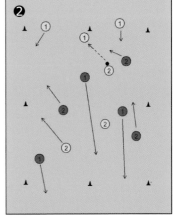

❸ Now the red team have just intercepted a pass and won back possession, so the Yellow Player Twos must drop out to their end of the playing area. If the ball goes out of the playing area, the coach can pass in another ball to the team who should have possession, or play can be restarted with a throw-in. Teams compete against each other to try and set a record for the length of time, or number of passes that can be completed.

Possible changes

■ Defenders could also be swapped automatically, if twenty passes are completed.

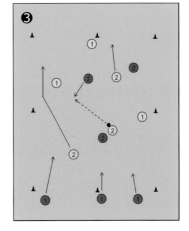

KNOCKOUT (WHIST) BALL

How it works

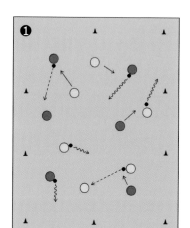

❶ The idea for this drill came from a card game we used to play as children, called Knockout Whist. During each round of the game you got one less card, hence one ball is removed during each round of this game. Red and yellow teams start with six versus six players in a large playing area, with three players in each team having possession of a ball. Play a possession game for thirty seconds or one minute, with each team trying to keep hold of as many balls as possible. Players without a ball can either try to offer support for a pass from their own team-mates, or try to tackle and win possession from an opposing player. If a ball goes outside the playing area it is lost for that round.

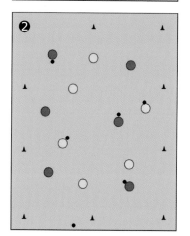

❷ The team that ends the time with possession of the most balls wins that round, in this case the red team. If each team has an equal number of balls, then the winners can be decided by any of the following means:

- a decision by the coach for the best piece of skill;
- the toss of a coin;
- a pass-off at a cone by a player from each team.

Or any other method you decide.

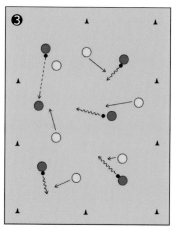

❸ One ball is left out, and the winning team starts the next round in possession of all five balls. Play a possession game for another thirty seconds or one-minute period, with each team again trying to keep hold of as many balls as possible. Keep playing, removing one ball at the end of each round, and the winning team starting in possession of all the balls that remain.

In the final round, the team that finishes with the ball at the end of the timed period wins the game. If the ball goes out of play, the coach can pass in another ball to the team that should be in possession.

ROB THE BANK

How it works

❶ The square at the bottom right is the bank and has balls, (gold bars), balanced on the cones, whilst the grid at the bottom left is a prison. Each red player is a robber and is given a number. The coach calls out any amount of numbers that they wish, in this case one, five and eight. These players try to run to the bank without being tagged by the yellow 'security guard'. If the yellow player tags a runner they must go to prison, as with Player Eight in this diagram. If they get to the bank, they can take a ball off a cone and attempt to dribble it back to the safety of the start line.

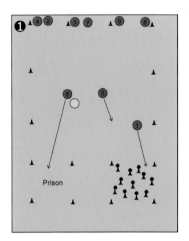

❷ Player One has decided to try and dribble the ball back alone. The yellow player, (security guard), must now try to tackle the ball from Player One and kick it out of the playing area. If this happens, Player One has to go back to the start line empty handed.

If Player One makes it back to the start line with the ball, (gold bar), they get to keep it for themselves. Player Five has decided to dribble the ball into the prison to set the other player free. (A player can only set free one other player from prison).

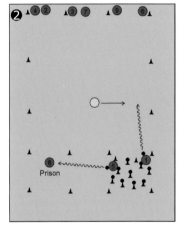

❸ They can now attempt to dribble or pass the ball between them, to get the gold bar safely back to the start line. If the yellow player tackles or intercepts the ball and kicks it out of the playing area, Player Five and Eight go back to the start line empty handed. If Player Five and Eight make it back to the start line with the ball, they get to share the gold bar between them. Play several rounds, calling out any amount of numbers you want to at a time. Then count up the players' gold bar tally to find a winner. Change the security guard and play a few more rounds.

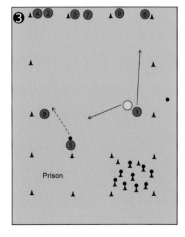

Possible changes

■ Play with two, or even three, security guards, calling out more numbers at any one time.
■ Any players tackled on the way back must also go to prison.

BALL RAIDERS 2

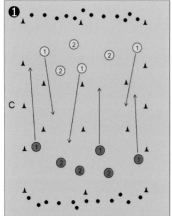

How it works

❶ Two teams start inside coned areas on each side, with lots of balls spread across each end of the playing area. There is also a central zone marked by the cones. Half of each team are Player Ones, and the other half Player Twos. On a signal from the coach, Player Ones must run across the other team's square to get a ball.

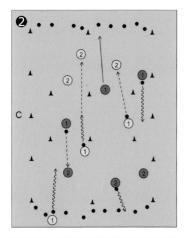

❷ They can then dribble a ball back across the playing area and into the central zone. From there they must pass the ball to a Player Two for them to turn, dribble and stop the ball behind the cones at their end. Player Ones can then run back again, to see if they can dribble and pass another ball back. No players are allowed to tackle, but if a player loses control of a ball and it goes outside the playing area, then it is lost for that round. Play for one or two minutes, then stop and count up the number of balls at each end to work out the winning team. Play again but this time Player Twos are the 'Ball Raiders'.

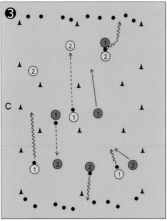

❸ **Possible changes**

Play again, but this time the Player Twos are allowed to tackle players from the other team. They are only allowed to tackle in that end area, and not in the central zone.

If they win a ball in the tackle, they can dribble and stop it behind the cones at their end of the playing area. The Player One who lost possession must run back to their end of the playing area, before returning to try and get another ball. Keep scores and change the roles of the players for the start of each new round.

END TO END

How it works

❶ Four yellow players start with the ball at one end of the playing area. A single red player stands in the opposing half, with three team-mates outside the playing area. The yellow players must try and keep possession of the ball, whilst trying to beat the red defender and stop the ball at the opposite end in line with the cones.

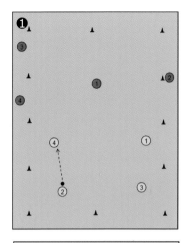

❷ When this happens, another red player comes in to make the teams four versus two. The yellow team now has to try and beat the two red defenders to get the ball back to the other end. If they do so, then another red player comes in to make it four versus three players and so on.

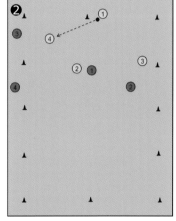

❸ When it gets to four versus four players, the yellow team keep trying to get from end to end, until they lose possession of the ball and a red defender kicks it out of the playing area. The red team then start with four players, against one opponent from the yellow team. Teams compete against each other to try and get the ball from one end to the other as many times as possible.

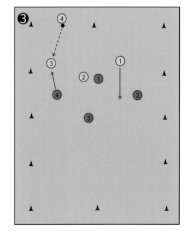

Possible changes

■ If the red team manages to get from one end to the other when it is four versus four, then the yellow team goes back down to three players and so on.

CONE RESCUE

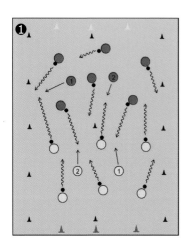

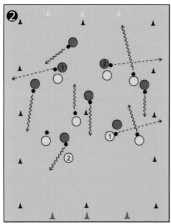

How it works

❶ Two teams start in opposite sides of the playing area. Most players in each team have a ball, but one or two players don't, depending on numbers of the whole group.

On a signal from the coach, the red and yellow teams have to try and capture and return a cone of their own colour, to their end of the playing area. Red and Yellow Players One and Two have to try and stop the opposing team from capturing and rescuing a cone.

❷ They do this by tackling opposing players and kicking their ball out of the playing area. That player then has to go and fetch their ball and re-enter the game, by dribbling the ball back in at their end of the playing area only, (not from the side).

❸ When a red or yellow player reaches the other end and picks up a cone, they must try and bring it back into their own half of the playing area. They do this by carrying it whilst dribbling. If they get into their own half of the playing area, the cone is rescued and can be placed at their end. If Player One or Two tackles them and kicks their ball out of the playing area, whilst carrying the cone, they must replace it. Only then can they run to fetch their ball, and re-enter the game as previously stated. The cone can be passed to another player on their team to rescue, as long as it is done before the player is tackled. Play until all one team's cones have been rescued, or for a certain time limit.

Possible changes

■ Play as a tagging only game at first. Keep one, two or three players, who are only allowed to tag opponents (depending on numbers), and the rest of the team trying to rescue the cones.

COACH IN THE MIDDLE

How it works

❶ Players are put into two equal teams. The yellow team have three players in each area, either side of the central zone. The red team has one player in each of those areas and two players at each end, who stand outside the playing area. Players must all stay in their own area. The coach stands in the central zone and starts the drill with a pass to one of the yellow players on either side. A player can take the role of the coach in the central zone if you wish.

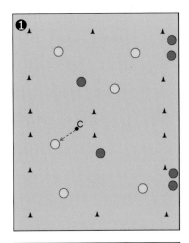

❷ Blue players must dribble, or pass, to keep possession of the ball within the playing area. The yellow players can pass the ball back to the coach in the central zone at any time.

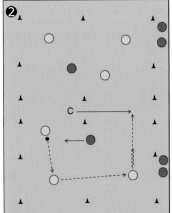

❸ The coach then turns and passes the ball to a yellow player on the other side of the central zone, where the yellow team again have to combine to keep possession of the ball. A blue player can pass directly back to the coach if they are under pressure, but every time the coach receives the ball, they turn and pass the ball into the other area. The red players on each side try to pressure the yellow team into making an error, or win possession of the ball and kick it out of the playing area. If this happens the two teams swap roles, changing the defender each time. The teams compete to make the largest number of passes before an error is made.

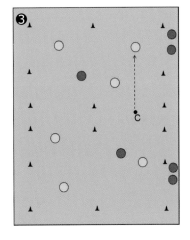

Possible changes

- Allow three errors before the teams swap, if they are losing possession quickly at first.
- Play four versus two, or three versus three players, depending on the age and ability of the group.

SNATCH

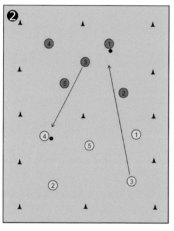

How it works

❶ Each team moves around their own square, dribbling and passing the ball between each other.

❷ The coach shouts a number, and that player must run quickly into the opposing team's square and try to win the ball. Set a twenty-second time limit for the Snatch to take place.

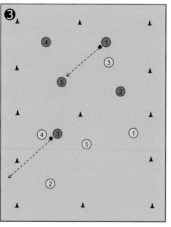

❸ If the player knocks the ball out of the playing area they score one point, but if the Snatcher manages to pass or dribble the ball back into their own team's square, they get three points. Play several rounds calling different numbers each time.

Possible changes

■ If you have a larger group, then each team could have two balls to pass around in their square.

■ You could also call more than one number of players to go into the opposing team's square to be Snatchers.

INVADER

How it works

❶ Two equal number teams start in both squares with a ball each, apart from one member of the team who becomes the Invader, and starts in the opposing team's square without a ball. Players with a ball dribble around their square and try to prevent the Invader from winning their ball. If the Invader wins a ball they have two options:

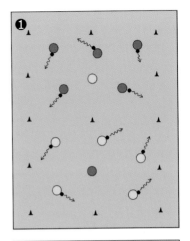

- knock the ball out of play, where it cannot be retrieved until the end of the game;
- pass the ball back to one of their own team in the other square.

❷ In this diagram, the Yellow Invader has won a ball from a red player and passes it back into his own team square. The Red Invader is challenging a yellow player for the ball, but they have passed it quickly to keep possession.

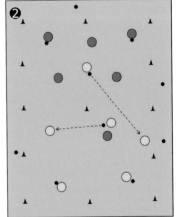

❸ The winning team is the one that keeps possession of at least one ball, the longest. Time how long the winning team can keep possession, and use that time to set a record to try and beat in future games. Play again with a different member of the team being the Invader.

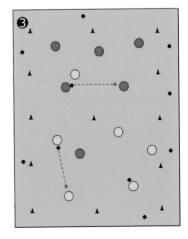

Possible changes

- The team that ends up with the last ball, has to complete five to ten passes to win the game. If the Invader wins the ball back before this happens, they can pass it back into their own team square. They then have to complete the same number of passes to win. If the ball goes out of the playing area in this time then the game is a draw.

POSSESSION SWITCHOVER

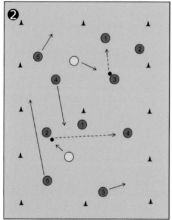

How it works

❶ Two teams start in each square, with a ball between them, and must pass the ball, keeping possession from the yellow defender. However, after passing the ball, the player must switch teams and run quickly into the other square to help them keep possession.

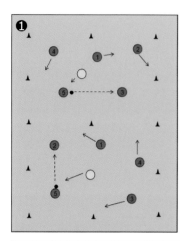

❷ In this diagram, Red Players Four and Five are switching over to the other squares after having made their passes.

❸ Red Players Four and Five have now switched over into the other squares of the channel. Red Players Two and Three are now switching as they have just made a pass. Players may not necessarily switch at the same time, depending on how the play goes in each square.

You may end up with seven red players in one square and only three in the other. If this happens, one of the team with fewer players may need to try and hold on to the ball, to allow more players to come in. If the red players lose possession then play can stop in both grids, or the other could attempt to continue whilst the ball was retrieved. Alternatively, another ball could be played in straight away by the coach. Play for two or three minutes then swap the blue defenders.

Possible changes

■ Make it easier by playing six or seven versus one, or with five or six versus two to make it harder, depending on the ability or numbers in the group.

POWERBALL

How it works

❶ Player Ones are attackers who each have a ball at their feet, whilst Player Twos are defenders standing inside the playing area. Several spare balls are placed just behind each end of the playing area. On a signal from the coach, red and yellow Player Ones dribble a ball into the playing area.

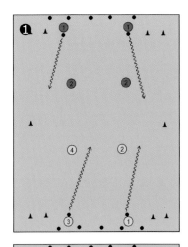

❷ Red Player Ones continue to dribble the ball, in an attempt to get past Yellow Player Twos. Yellow Player Ones continue to dribble the ball in an attempt to get past Red Player Twos. Defenders have to try and force the attackers into a mistake to lose control of the ball, or tackle them, so that the ball leaves the playing area. All players are allowed in any part of the playing area.

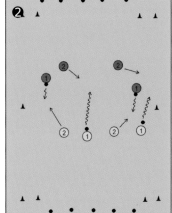

❸ If Player Ones get past the defender, they must dribble the ball between the cone goals at each corner of the playing area to score a point. They then keep the same ball and try and do the same thing going back in the opposite direction. If Player One's ball is lost or kicked out of the playing area, they must continue running to the end without a ball. They then get a spare ball and try to beat the defender coming back in the opposite direction. Play for two or three minutes and then swap roles. The winning team/individual, is the one who scores the most points.

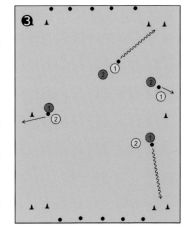

Possible changes

■ Play it with two versus two players, where the defenders are allowed to tackle any player on the other team, or match pairs up one versus one, so each Red Player One can only be tackled by the same Yellow Player Two.

■ Have another team(s) resting at the side of the playing area, and play as a round-robin or knockout competition.

FOUR GOAL TAKE-AWAY

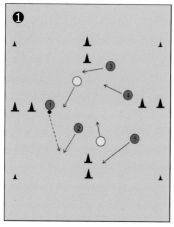

How it works

❶ A large area is set up with four small cone goals, one close to each corner of the playing space. The red players are the attacking team and have to try and keep possession from the two yellow defenders. Red Player One has passed the ball into the space ahead of Red Player Two, and then moved to the opposite side of the cone goal.

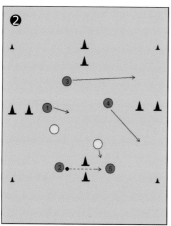

❷ Red Player Two then passes the ball back to Red Player One, through the cone goal to score a point. Play continues with the red players attempting to keep possession, but also trying to score as many points as possible by passing the ball through any of the cone goals. If the ball goes out of the playing area, the coach can quickly play in another ball to a red player in space. If the yellow defenders gain possession, then the red team could lose a point. Play for two or three minutes and then change the yellow defenders. Can the next team beat the point score?

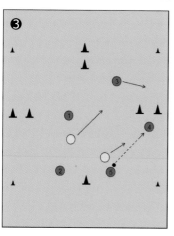

❸ Possible changes

■ Make it easier by playing five versus one, or six or seven versus two, or with five or six versus three, to make it harder.

■ After a goal is scored through one of the cone goals, it could be removed by the coach, as shown in this diagram. Can the red players score in all four goals without losing possession?

■ If the yellow team gain possession, they could try to score through one of the cone goals to end the game, the red team then losing all the points they might have gained.

THREE GOAL GAME

How it works

❶ Red and yellow teams play a four versus four game within the playing area, whilst a fifth player stands behind the three goals at each opposite end. Normal rules apply, as the two teams try to score in any of the three small cone goals at each end of the playing area. The players at each end can move from one goal to another, as long as they stay behind the line of the cones.

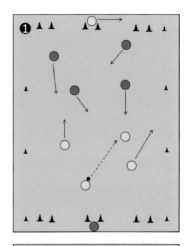

❷ In order to score a goal, the player behind the goals must move in line and stop the ball between the cones, or just behind the cone goal for it to count. The player who supplied the pass then swaps places with the player behind the goals.

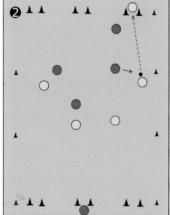

❸ Play then continues with a red player passing the ball from just in front of the same goal.

Possible changes

■ The cone goal can be removed once it has been scored in, so that a team must score through each of the three goals to win the game.

■ Play without the player behind the goals and just pass through any of the goals to score.

■ You can play any numbers on each side and have any number of goals.

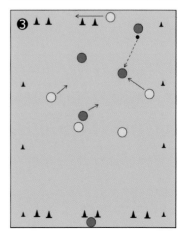

TRIPLE TARGET

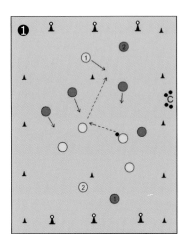

How it works

❶ Four players from each team play against each other, but are only allowed in the central zone. Player Ones from each team are attackers, whilst Player Twos from each team are defenders. They are only allowed in the smaller zones at each end of the playing area. There are three cones at each end with a ball balanced on top, which make up the triple targets. The yellow team are in possession and have to try and pass the ball to their attacker in the end zone.

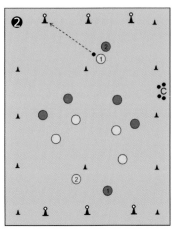

❷ The yellow attacker has to try and knock one of the balls off a cone to score. They are allowed to pass the ball back to a team-mate in the central zone if needed. The red defender attempts to tackle or block the shot. If the red defender wins possession, then they have to try and pass the ball to one of their team in the central zone.

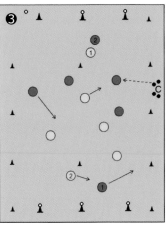

❸ The yellow team score a point if a ball is knocked off a cone, but only have two targets left to attempt to score. The coach can then pass another ball to a player in the central zone to restart the game.

Possible changes

- The ball can be replaced on top of the cone, so there are always three targets.
- One extra player is allowed to join Player Ones in the end zones, to make a two versus one when trying to score.
- After receiving a pass, Player Ones can lay the ball back to a yellow team-mate, for them to shoot first time to knock a ball off and score.
- Play with just a single cone goal at each end.

QUICK CHANGE

How it works

❶ The red and yellow teams play a four versus four, normal rules game, within the playing area, whilst a third blue team wait ready, just outside the playing area. No goalkeepers are required.

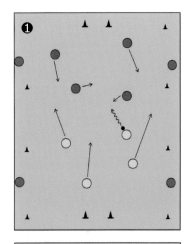

❷ At any time the coach can call a colour, (in this case yellow), and that team has to leave the field of play immediately to be replaced by the team that is off the field. The team coming on has to organize themselves quickly to defend or gain possession of the ball, before the team still on the field can take advantage and score. The team which scores the most goals whilst on the field of play wins the game.

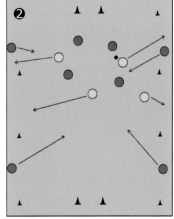

❸ **Possible changes**
- Play with four versus four players, but each colour has two teams, one on the field of play and one at the side. When the coach shouts 'Change!' the two halves of the team have to swap on and off the field immediately.
- Play with goalkeepers if you wish.

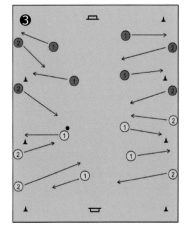

HEAD TO SCORE

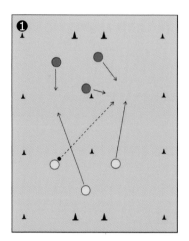

How it works

❶Play three versus three with normal game rules, but no goalkeepers and a playing area divided into thirds by cones.

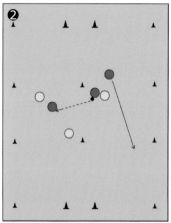

❷In this diagram, the red team have won possession of the ball and will try to score in the yellow goal.

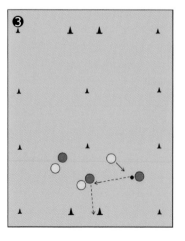

❸Once a team gets the ball into the final third of the playing area, any of them can pick the ball up and throw it for a team member to attempt to score a headed goal.

Possible changes

■ Play any number of players on each side, but the smaller the teams, the more players get to practise heading for goal.

■ Give five points for a headed goal, but also one point for a goal scored with the feet.

SCORE IN THE MIDDLE

How it works

❶ Red and yellow teams play with six versus six players inside the large playing area. However, the teams are split equally, either side of a central goal, with a neutral goalkeeper. Players must stay within their own half of the playing area.

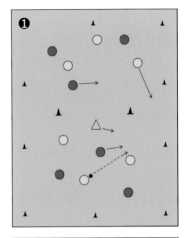

❷ Normal rules apply, except the players are allowed to pass the ball from one side of the goal to the other, as shown in the diagram.

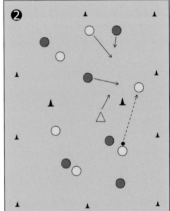

❸ The yellow team have now created an opening to score, after passing the ball to the other side. When a goal is scored, play can either be restarted by the goalkeeper throwing the ball out, or by the non-scoring team gaining possession at the far end of the playing area.

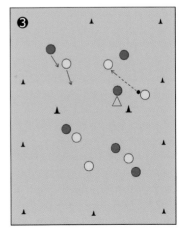

Possible changes

■ Play three versus two players on either side of the goal, to make it easier for the attacking team.

■ Allow all, or just nominated, players to move freely from one side of the goal to the other.

■ Play with two balls, starting at the same time, from each end of the playing area.

■ If you're feeling really adventurous, play with two goalkeepers, one for each team. Or set up a triangular goal in the middle and have three goalkeepers!

CHAPTER 3

Circle Drills

Many of the early drills from Chapter 1, can be quite easily adapted to work just as well in this circular playing area. Including these will give you greater variety of practises to use, so that your entire session can be easily planned around the one, single, multipurpose cone set-up. Keep things simple for yourself, and your players so that you can all enjoy, and get maximum benefit from, the sessions that you plan.

Creating stories around your drills can also be a great motivating factor in getting the most out of your sessions. Many activities and games within this book are based around the theme from a film or television programme that was popular at the time of coaching. It is amazing how much interest and excitement you can create around what might, otherwise, be perceived as a fairly ordinary, run of the mill practise. It's still up to you, however, to sell the idea, so take the time to enjoy setting the scene and be up for a bit of role play to make the most of the story. The more effort you put in, the more fun and enjoyment you'll get out.

To set up your circle, first place a cone in the centre of your playing area. Walk out ten, fifteen or twenty paces from this central cone, depending on how big you want the playing area to be, and put down another cone. Repeat this process so that you have a cone at twelve, three, six and nine 'o' clock from the centre. You can then pace out each of the other hour times, or just estimate the distance by using your four markers as a guide.

Or, if you're really stuck for time to set up your playing area, try this method out. Give each player a cone and get together to form a small circle in the middle of your playing area. Get all of them to face outwards, stride out a set number of paces and then put the cone down on the ground. It might not end up perfect, but will certainly give you a quick, usable area to work in.

POSSIBLE SESSIONS

The following selections are only suggestions of how drills could be combined, to create a one, or two-hour session. As a teacher, or coach, you need to assess the ability of your group and take into account possible numbers, before making appropriate choices of your own. All these sessions could also be started with a warm-up of your own, and ended with some regular small-sided games.

- Dobbie's Master
- Starfish
- Top Gun

- Catch Up

- Finding Nemo
- Treasure Hunters
- Close the Gate
- Umbrella Game

- Cone Playground
- Cone Raiders
- Circle Races

- Chain Gang (Chapter 2)
- Pinball
- On Your Toes
- Passing Triangle
- Bermuda Triangle

DOBBIE'S MASTER

How it works

❶ All players dribble a ball inside the smallest of the two cone circles. All the players are 'Dobbie' (the servant character from Harry Potter), who must obey only their master and no one else. The coach calls out instructions such as the following:

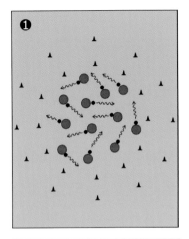

- Master says sit on your ball;
- Master says stop;
- Master says use your left foot only;
- Master says pick up the ball.

The red players, (Dobbies), must follow these instructions as the Master has said them. However, if the coach just says: 'stop' or 'pick up the ball', then they should ignore these and carry on dribbling their ball.

❷ If a player makes a mistake and follows an instruction that is not given by the master, then they must go into the outer circle.

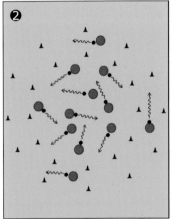

❸ If that player makes another mistake, then they must dribble their ball outside the large circle. However, if they ignore the next instruction that isn't from the master, then they can come back into the inner circle. Players remain on the outside of both circles if they continue to make errors. Which players can be in the inner circle at the end of the game? Can any player stay in the inner circle all the way through a five-minute, warm-up game?

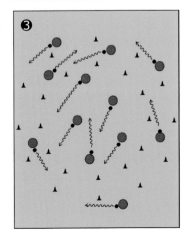

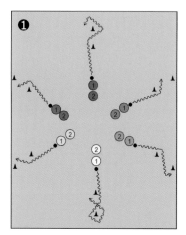

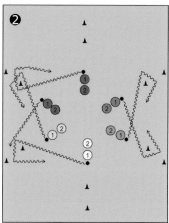

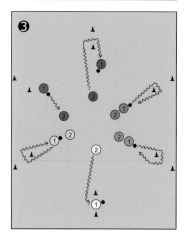

STARFISH

How it works
❶ Player Ones dribble the ball out to their cone gate, on a signal from the coach, and have to do the following depending on the number called:

- One – dribble to touch the first cone and then back to their partner;
- Two – dribble to touch the second cone and then back to their partner;
- Three – dribble to touch both cones, returning to their partner after each one;
- Four – dribble the ball in a figure of eight pattern around the cones and then back to their partner, (as shown in the diagram);
- Five – dribble the ball through the cone gate and pass back to their partner.

❷
- Six – dribble the ball through any other cone gate apart from their own, (as shown in the diagram).
- Seven – dribble the ball through their own gate and then every other gate around the circle before going back through their own gate and returning to partner.

❸
- Eight – dribble to the cone gate, perform ten actions of any skill, for example, toe taps/ instep touches and return to their partner.

Player Two performs the same skill and partners compete to finish first.

Possible changes
- Start without the ball doing running relays.
- Any other dribbling/passing skills, or fun elements you want to include.

CONE PLAYGROUND

How it works

❶ Different coloured cones are set up in a large circular playing area, as shown in the diagram. Firstly, players jog/run around inside the area avoiding all the cones.

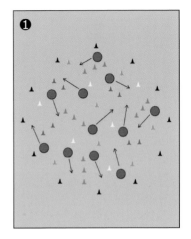

❷ The coach then demonstrates an action to do when players arrive at the following colour cones:

- White – perform a two-footed to two-footed jump over the cone;
- Orange – stop and turn quickly in a different direction;
- Blue – run a figure of eight around the pair of cones;
- Green – run a zigzag pattern through the three cones.

If you are doing this practise with younger players, you may wish to stop them and demonstrate one co-lour at a time, having them practise just that action before introducing another. The coach could then call out one or more colours, and the players can only go to that/those colour(s) to perform the actions.

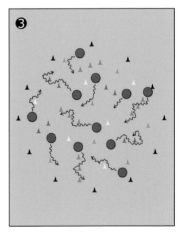

❸ Repeat the same practise, but this time whilst dribbling a ball. This time at the white cone, stop the ball and grip it tight between the feet, whilst performing a two-footed to two-footed jump over the cone, or flick the ball over the cone.

Possible changes

- Add another colour with a different action, or com-pletely change the actions performed.
- Demonstrate a specific type of turn to perform at the orange cone, or zigzag through the green cones by pushing the ball with the outside of the left and right feet.
- Make it more competitive by earning points for demonstrating good skills.
- Do it in pairs, both having a ball, or the leader hav-ing a ball and changing over at regular intervals.

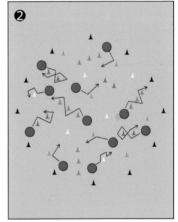

CONE RAIDERS

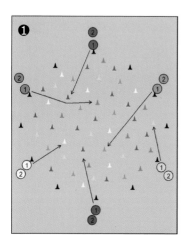

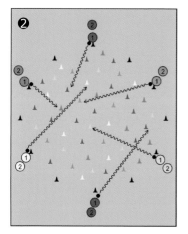

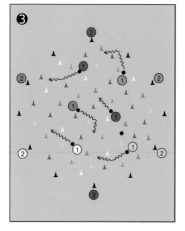

How it works

❶ You need lots of different coloured cones for this one! On a signal from the coach, Player Ones run out to knock down a cone of their own colour. They must then run back to tag their partner, who knocks down a different cone and so on. (If the cones are small, they can turn them over instead of knocking them down). The first pair to knock down all of their cones are the winners. Then repeat, but putting the cones back up, (or turning them back over). Then give the teams one minute to knock down as many cones, which are not their colour, as they can. As soon as a team's cones are all knocked down, they are out of the game.

❷ This time repeat the same, but dribbling a ball and putting the cones back up, (or turning them back over). Then give the teams two minutes to knock down as many cones, which are not their colour, as they can, whilst dribbling their ball. As soon as a team's cones are all knocked down, they are out of the game. Finally, have a race to pick up a cone of their own colour and bring it back to their starting point.

❸ Possible changes

■ When collecting the cones in at the end, have all Player Ones dribbling within the playing area. The coach shouts out a colour and players have to pick a cone of that colour, as quickly as possible, and take it back to their partner. Then repeat for Player Twos. As you go on there will not be enough cones for each player, so you may need to warn players not to compete for cones too strongly!

FINDING NEMO

How it works

❶ Hide 'Nemo', (a toy fish), underneath one of the tall cones in the centre of the circle, surrounded by a small circle of balls, or round cones. The yellow players are the sharks, protecting the cones in the centre of the playing area. The red players are Nemo's friends trying to rescue him. On a signal from the coach, the red players can try to run into the centre without being tagged. If tagged, the player must return to the outside and wait until the next turn.

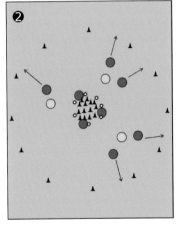

❷ If a red player gets to the middle, they are safe and can lift up one cone to try and find Nemo. If Nemo is not found, the players have to try and run back to the outside of the circle, (with the cone), without being tagged. If they make it, there is one less cone to search under, but if they get tagged the cone is replaced back in the centre. (You can shuffle them around if you want).

   If one of the players finds Nemo, then they must get back to the outside of the circle, without being tagged, in order to rescue him. If tagged, the coach hides Nemo back under a cone, for the game to continue on his next signal. Change the sharks if Nemo is rescued, and challenge them to guard him more safely, in other words for the red players to take more turns or cones lifted for Nemo to be rescued.

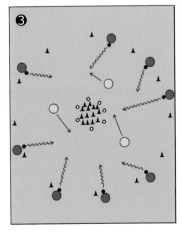

❸ Now the red players start with a ball and must dribble to the coned area in the centre of the circle. They must stop the ball within the safe area to lift a cone. The sharks try to kick their ball out of the circle, to make them go back to the start, or to stop them getting back to the outside with Nemo.

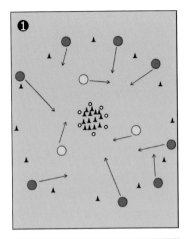

Possible changes

■ If more than one player gets to the middle when Nemo is found, they could swap possession of the toy to confuse the sharks.

■ The player who finds Nemo could also pass their ball to the outside of the circle, for another player to control in order to rescue him.

CATCH UP

How it works

❶ Players spread out around the edge of a circular playing area. The coach calls out two numbers and those players have to swap places, the second player called attempting to beat the first player to their place. In the diagram, Player Nine was called first, then Player Five. Player Nine must have been ready and listening, as they look like getting there first.

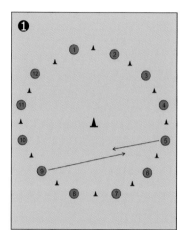

❷ Repeat, but the players must run into the centre and touch the cone before trying to get to the other player's place first. In this diagram, Player One was called first but was not on their toes and as ready to go as Player Six. Even though they were called second, it looks like Player Six will get there first.

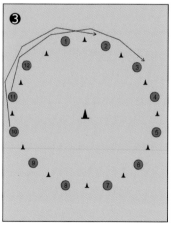

❸ Repeat, but calling out numbers next to each other, with the higher number first. The first player called must run clockwise around the outside of the circle, and the second player has to try and catch them before they get round the circle. In this diagram, Player Eleven was called first and has made a good start, being well ahead. Player Ten is still chasing hard to catch up. Player Eleven has to get back to his/her own place before being caught.

Possible changes

■ All these chasing/catching activities can then be done whilst dribbling a ball.

CIRCLE RACES

How it works

❶ Player pairs stand evenly spaced around the circle. On a signal from the coach, Player Two starts by crawling between the legs of Player One, running to the middle of the circle and then back between Player One's legs to finish. Change round player roles and repeat.

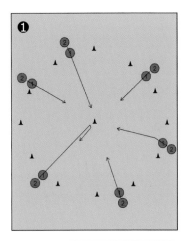

❷ Do the same again, but this time players have to run around the outside of the circle. Possibilities are endless but here are just a few suggestions such as:

- run and touch any four cones in the circle;
- run and crawl through two other players' legs;
- run around the player on the opposite side of the circle.

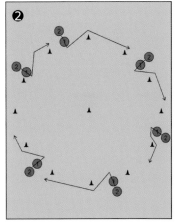

❸ Possible changes

- All, or a selection of, these races can then be repeated whilst dribbling a ball.
- The ball can be passed through their partner's legs to start and finish each race.

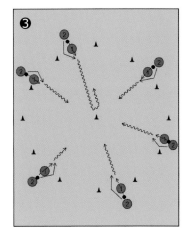

TREASURE HUNTERS

How it works

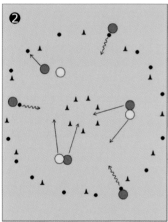

❶ A group of red players, (treasure hunters), start inside the centre circle. Balls, (treasure), are placed around the edge of the outer circle, with several defenders, (guards), in between. On a signal from the coach, the red players must try and get past the defenders to get to a ball.

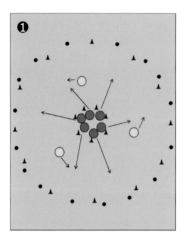

❷ If a red player is tagged on the way to grabbing some treasure, (ball), they must return to the centre circle and stay there until all the other red players return. If a red player gets to a ball, they must try and dribble it back to the safety of the inner circle.

❸ If a red player reaches the inner circle with control of the ball, then the treasure is safe. If a guard, (yellow player), tackles and wins the ball, they must try and dribble it back to the edge of the outer circle. Until it is safely stopped there, the treasure hunter, (red player), can still try and win back possession of the ball. A red player cannot be tackled if they stand still with their foot on the ball. Yellow players must retreat to at least three metres.

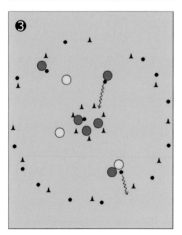

Once all the treasure hunters have returned, with or without some treasure, the coach gives another signal for the next round to begin. How many balls can the red team get to the middle in five or ten rounds? Change roles and play the game again.

Possible changes

■ If a red player gets a ball to the safety of the inner circle, they are allowed back out to help others get their ball to the middle by being available for a pass.

SUPERHEROES TO THE RESCUE

How it works

❶ A group of red players, (thieves/criminals), start inside the centre circle. Yellow players dribble a ball within the outer circle. On a signal from the coach, the red players must try and steal a ball from a yellow player and get it back to the centre circle. Two blue players, (superheroes), try to help any yellow player keep possession of the ball. The blue players could choose any superhero character they want.

❷ In this diagram, one of the blue players is acting as a screen for a yellow player to move away from danger. The other blue player is trying to help win back possession of a ball for a yellow player. If successful the yellow player can continue dribbling in the circle. Another red player has stolen a ball and is dribbling it into the safety of the centre circle. They can leave the ball there and go out to try and steal another ball.

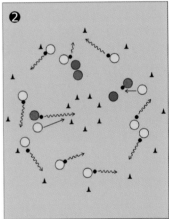

❸ The yellow player who has had their ball stolen must then leave the playing area, to stand outside the circle. How many balls can the thieves, (red team), steal within a certain time limit? Change roles and play another game.

Possible changes

■ Allow yellow players to become extra guards when their ball is lost.
■ Allow yellow players around the circle to be available for a pass, if under pressure from a red player inside the circle. When the ball is passed, the player on the outside takes possession and dribbles the ball in, whilst the player who passed the ball takes their place on the outside of the circle.

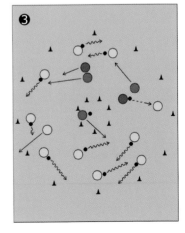

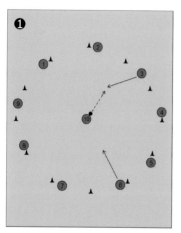

CIRCLE POSSESSION

How it works

❶ Players spread out around the edge of a circular playing area. One player stands in the middle of the circle with a ball. The coach calls out two numbers and those players have to enter the playing area. In the diagram, Player Three and Player Six have been called first, and so enter the playing area to help Player Ten keep possession of the ball.

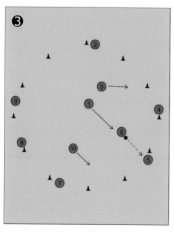

❷ The coach then shouts a third number, (Player One), and that player also enters the playing area to try and win possession of the ball. The players in the middle must try and keep possession of the ball from the one defender. The red players can either pass to each other, or to any of the other players around the edge of the circle.

❸ The red team only score a point for a pass made between the three of them, inside the circle. As mentioned, they can pass to a player on the outside of the circle, but do not gain a point for doing so. The yellow player must try to tackle, or intercept, the ball and kick it out of the playing area to end the game. That player then starts with the ball in the middle of the circle to begin another round. Each group tries to beat the points total scored previously.

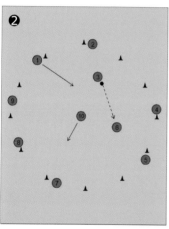

Possible changes

■ Play with two or more defenders, depending on the number and ability of the players. Each player could have a bib/pinny on the ground behind them, around the edge of the circle. The defenders have to put this on, before coming into the circle to try and win the ball.

CLOSE THE GATE

How it works

❶ The red players have a ball each, and must try and keep possession of their own ball. The yellow players must try and pressure the red players and kick their ball out of the playing area. Red players are allowed to dribble out of the playing area, but only through one of the larger cone gates spaced out around the edge of the circle. Yellow players cannot leave the playing area.

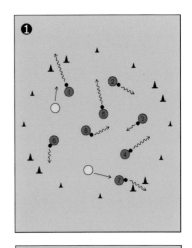

❷ In this diagram, Red players One and Seven have escaped out of a cone gate and are dribbling around the outside of the circle, to re-enter the playing area through different gates. Red player Five has had their ball kicked out of the playing area. The player must retrieve the ball and re-enter through a cone gate. Red player Eight is under pressure from a yellow player, so has turned towards a cone gate to escape to safety if necessary.

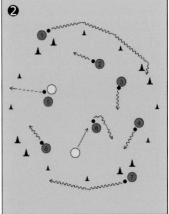

❸ Play for one or two minutes, then swap two red players with the yellow players. They then have to try and kick more balls out of the playing area than the previous pair. Play until all of the group have taken the role of the yellow players.

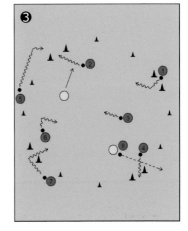

Possible changes

- Play five versus three players, depending on the age or ability of the group. If you play with a larger group, make sure you have more cone gates than yellow players.
- When a red player has their ball kicked out, they are not allowed to retrieve it but can offer support to other red players, to help keep possession of their ball.

AROUND THE WORLD

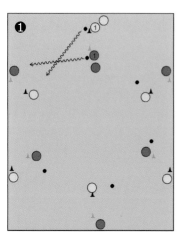

How it works

❶ Set out an inner and an outer circle of cones, about four or five metres apart, using different colours, as shown on the diagram. Red and Yellow Player One start by dribbling the ball towards the next player in their team, around the outside of the circle. (Take care when crossing over).

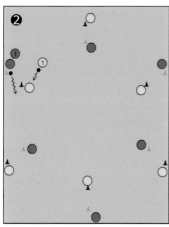

❷ Players continue to dribble the ball around the circle as a team. The first team to get the ball twice around the circle, and back to the start, wins. How many cones can the team get the ball round in one or two minutes?

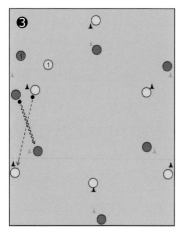

❸ **Possible changes**
- Start with a crossover running relay, before dribbling the ball.
- Players can pass the ball to the next person in the relay, but run the risk of hitting the player from the other team, who may be crossing their path.
- Have one team start dribbling/passing around the outside circle. When halfway round, start the other team doing the same around the inside circle – how quickly can they catch up? Swap over.
- Start two different balls going at different sides of the circle.

AROUND THE WORLD 2

How it works

❶ Red player One starts by dribbling the ball towards the next cone gate in the circle.

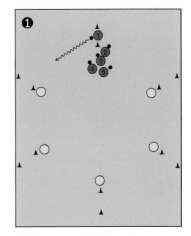

❷ Red player One passes the ball to the blue player at the inside of the circle, and then continues their run through the cone gate.

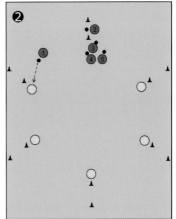

❸ Red Player One receives the ball back from the yellow player at the inside of the circle, and then continues to dribble to the next cone gate to repeat the sequence. Red Player Two then sets off around the circle, and the other red players continue to set off in turn. The teams then swap over.

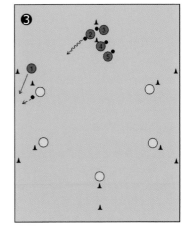

Possible changes

■ Yellow players stand in between the cones at the gates and lay-off the ball to either the outside, or the inside, of the circle for the red player to run on to and continue to the next gate.

■ Yellow players pass straight back to the red player, for them to control through the gate with their first touch, before moving on.

■ Yellow players pick up the ball and feed it back to the red player in the air, for them to control through the gate before moving on.

TOP GUN

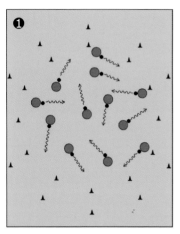

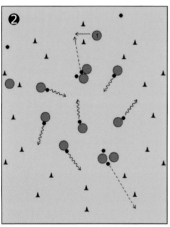

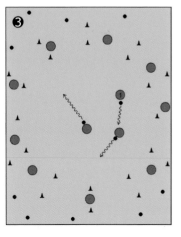

How it works

❶ Players have a ball each and dribble around inside the playing area, keeping control of the ball and their heads up. The idea of the game is to keep control of your own ball, whilst also trying to kick the ball of another player out of the playing area.

❷ If a player's ball is kicked out, they must go into the outside area. Player One has managed to intercept a ball that another player has tried to kick out, or just lost control of, and so can get back into the game with that ball.

❸ If the players get too defensive when there are only two or three of them left, set a time limit for a player to make a move, or else they are out. All the players around the outside can still get back into the game, if they intercept a ball being kicked out of the area. The winner, (Top Gun), is the last player left in with a ball.

Possible changes

■ Don't have an outer area, and when players lose their ball they are just out of the game altogether.

DEMENTORS

How it works

❶ Red players spread out within the playing area. Outside are three yellow players, (Dementors), and four cones, with a ball balanced on each one. On a signal from the coach, one of the Dementors is allowed to enter the area and attempt to tag the red players. If tagged, the red player must drop to the ground, as if drained of life by the Dementor.

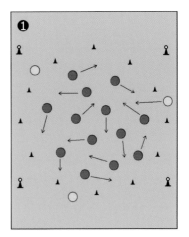

❷ At any time during the game, one of the red players can run out of the playing area and attempt to retrieve a ball. If they get back with the ball and shout: 'Patronus', then all the players who are down are released from the spell and the Dementor is cast out of the circle. The coach then gives a signal for a different yellow player to go into the circle and start catching them again.

However, if the red player is tagged by one of the yellow players outside the circle, then they too must drop to the ground. At any time the coach can call for a second Dementor to go into the circle. The game ends when all the balls, (spells), have been used and all the red players have been caught.

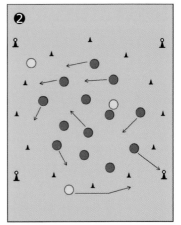

❸ This time each red player has a ball, (wand), that they must keep safe. The Dementor coming into the circle must tackle the ball, (snatch the wand), and kick it out of the playing area. Any red player who loses their ball must drop down as before. To cast a Patronus Spell, a red player must risk trying to knock one of the balls off a cone, with a pass from inside the playing area. However, the yellow players can attempt to intercept any pass.

If successful, all the red players can get their ball back and the Dementors have to start again. The game ends when all the balls, (spells), have been used and all the red players have had their ball kicked out of the playing area.

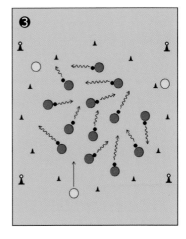

Possible changes

■ Allow the red players who have had their ball kicked out, to stay alive and support other players, to help them keep possession of a ball.

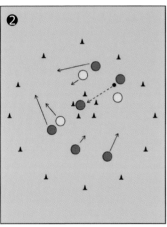

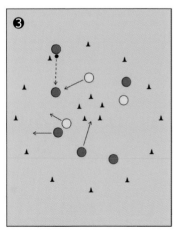

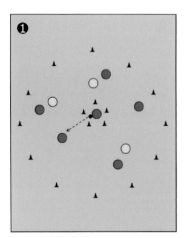

SAFETY CIRCLE

How it works

❶ The red player in the 'Safety Circle' starts the game by passing the ball to another of their team-mates. When the ball has been passed, the red player must move out of the small centre circle. The red players try to keep possession of the ball for as long as possible. Yellow players can move anywhere, except within the 'Safety Circle', in the centre of the playing area.

❷ Any red player can dribble the ball into the 'Safety Circle' at any time, to escape pressure from a yellow defender. A different red player can also move into the 'Safety Circle' to receive a pass, without being challenged by a yellow player.

❸ If the ball goes out of the playing area, then play re-starts with another pass from the 'Safety Circle' by a red player. Rotate the players so that they all have a turn at being the defending team. Teams compete to try and beat a previous record of time in possession, or number of passes completed.

Possible changes

■ Limit the number of times a team can use the 'Safety Circle', within a single possession, or within a certain time.

■ Make it easier, or harder, to keep possession by de-creasing, or increasing, the number of defenders.

UMBRELLA GAME

How it works

❶ Why the Umbrella game you may ask? Well this idea came to me when I was taking an Under Eleven school team to an outdoor, five-a-side, soccer tournament. The start was delayed and so we found a spare area of grass, stuck my umbrella in the ground and played a four versus two, possession game and then a three versus three, small-sided game, with no coned playing area, trying to hit the umbrella. The kids loved it and I've used it ever since.

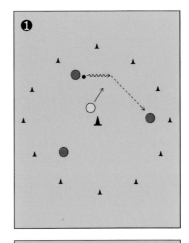

Three red players try to keep possession of the ball against one blue player. They can dribble or pass anywhere within the circular playing area. If the yellow player wins the ball, or kicks it out of the playing area, then they swap with the red player who made the mistake.

❷ The red players score by passing the ball to hit a taller cone in the centre of the circle. If they achieve this, then the yellow player stays as the defender. If the red players score three times, then swap the defender.

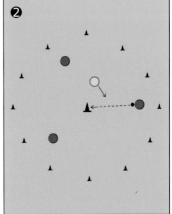

❸ Set up a small, coned, circular exclusion zone around the central cone, if the defender insists on standing next to the cone all the time.

Possible changes

■ Play four versus one, or five versus two players, depending on the age and ability of the group.
■ Play three versus three players as a small-sided game. If a team hits the central cone, they keep possession and restart the game anywhere around the edge of the circle.

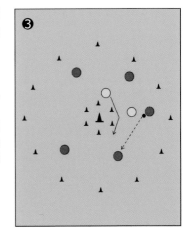

PASSING TRIANGLE

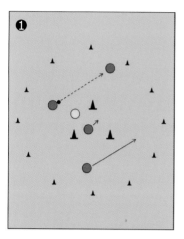

How it works

❶ One red player must stay inside the triangle, set up in the centre of the circular playing area. The other red players, and one yellow defender, are allowed anywhere in the circle, apart from inside the central triangle. The red players try to keep possession of the ball. They get one point for a pass to a team-mate in the circle.

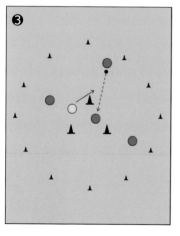

❷ If the yellow defender intercepts, or tackles, the ball and kicks it out of the area, then the red players must start their points count again. This also happens if the red players allow the ball to go out of the circular playing area by mistake.

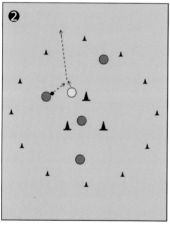

❸ If the red players pass to the player in the central triangle, then they get a bonus five points, but the ball must be controlled inside the triangle. Play for three or four minutes, attempting to beat previous best scores, and then change the roles of the players.

Possible changes

■ Make it easier by playing four versus one within the outer circle, or three versus two to make it harder.
■ Restrict the players to two touches on the ball, and/or the yellow defender is only allowed to intercept passes, but not make tackles.
■ Have no red player in the central triangle at the start, and allow any of the players to make a move into the triangle to receive a pass for five points.

BERMUDA TRIANGLE

How it works

❶ Start with five or six red players against a yellow defender. Only the red players are allowed to go inside the central triangle. The red players try to keep possession of the ball.

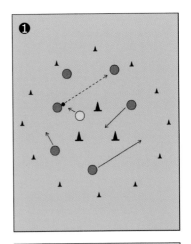

❷ They have to try and pass the ball into the central triangle for one of them to control. If they achieve this, that red player 'disappears' out of the game and stands outside the circle.

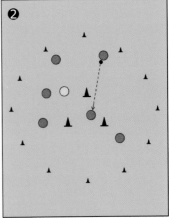

❸ A different red player continues the game, by passing the ball in from the central triangle. If the yellow defender intercepts, or tackles, the ball and kicks it out of the area, then the red players must start again and all the players come back into the game. This also happens if the red players allow the ball to go out of the circular playing area by mistake. The last player has to dribble the ball from the centre, around any outside cone and back into the middle, to finish the game and have all players disappear inside the Bermuda Triangle.

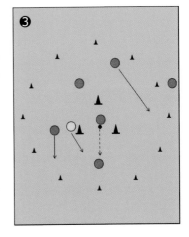

Possible changes

■ Play with two yellow defenders to add greater challenge.

■ Players are only allowed two touches on the ball.

KNOCKDOWN

How it works

❶ The red players try to knock down the cones in the centre of the circle. They can move around the edge of the playing area and pass anywhere across the circle, in order to try and create an opportunity to pass, or shoot, at one of the cones.

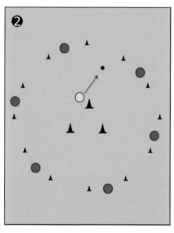

❷ The yellow player can try to intercept passes across the circle, but may risk leaving the cones undefended. If the yellow player intercepts a pass across the circle, then they swap with the red player who made the mistake.

❸ If the red players knock down a cone, then it is put back up and the red team continue to see how many they can knock down without any interceptions. If the red players miss a cone, but keep possession of the ball, then play continues.

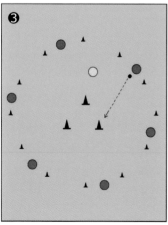

Possible changes

- ■ The cones are left down and the red team has to try and knock down all three, without losing possession.
- ■ Enlarge the circle and/or widen the distance between the centre cones and have two yellow players inside defending.
- ■ Put one of the red players into the middle, as well as those around the edge. This player is allowed to pass to other red players, but not pass to knock down any of the cones.

KNOCKDOWN 2

How it works

❶ Red players try to keep possession of the ball against one yellow defender. They can move anywhere inside the circular playing area, to try and create an opportunity to pass/shoot to knock down one of the cones. The yellow player can try to intercept passes across the circle, but may risk leaving the cones undefended. If the yellow player intercepts a pass across the circle, then they swap with the red player who made the mistake.

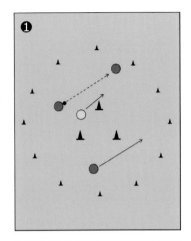

❷ If the red players knock down a cone, then it is put back up and the red team continue to see how many they can knock down without any interceptions. If the red players miss a cone, but keep possession of the ball, then play continues.

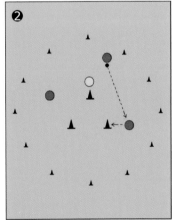

❸ Possible changes

- Add another red player to make it four versus one.
- Enlarge the circle, widening the distance between the centre cones, and play six or seven versus two.
- The red players score bonus points by passing to each other through the triangle, without knocking down a cone, (as shown in this diagram).

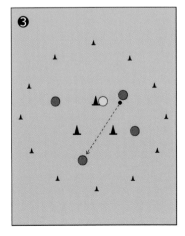

MIDDLE PLAYER SWITCH

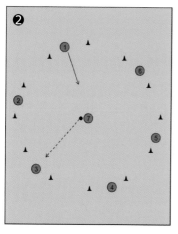

How it works

❶ Players stand evenly spaced around the circle. Player One starts by passing the ball to Player Seven, in the middle of the circle.

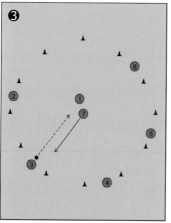

❷ Player Seven controls the ball and passes to any other red player on the outside of the circle. Player One follows their pass, to take the place of Player Seven in the middle of the circle.

❸ Player Three then passes to Player One, who has taken up the position in the middle of the circle. Player Seven follows their pass, to fill the space that Player Three will leave when they follow their pass into the middle of the circle. Players continue to pass and follow this pattern. Challenge the players to continue for one or two minutes without any errors, or to attempt to make between ten and twelve passes within a minute, then try to beat this target.

Possible changes

■ Players can dribble and stop the ball in the same sequence as a warm-up, before trying it passing.
■ First touch passes only.

PINBALL

How it works

❶ Players spread out around the edge of a circular playing area. Red Player One dribbles the ball towards the central cone, turns and looks up. They can then pass to any other red player on the outside of the circle, in this case Red Player Two.

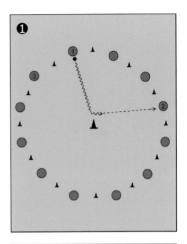

❷ Red Player Two then dribbles the ball into the centre and passes to another red player on the outside of the circle, in this case Red Player Three. Red Player One follows their pass and takes the place of Red Player Two on the outside of the circle. Red Player Three continues this dribbling and passing sequence. It is important that all players call the name of the player they are going to pass to.

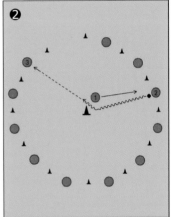

❸ Add in another ball after thirty seconds or one minute. Allow the group a short while to practise with the two balls, then challenge them to go thirty seconds or one minute with no errors. If they're not successful, try again. If they are successful, add another ball. Allow time to practise and then challenge the group again. The number of balls that can be kept going will vary, depending on the size and ability of the group.

Possible changes

■ For younger or lower ability groups, players can dribble the ball into the centre, and then continue dribbling the ball to a player on the outside of the circle. They then stop the ball for the next player to dribble into the centre, and take their place on the outside of the circle. In this case, add at least one other ball fairly quickly, otherwise a lot of players will be standing around for a long time waiting for a turn.

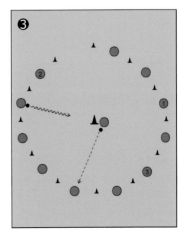

PRESSURE PASSING

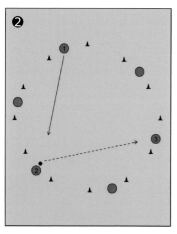

How it works

❶ Players stand evenly spaced around the circle. Player One starts by passing the ball to any other player in the circle, in this case Player Two.

❷ Player One then follows the pass, to put pressure on Player Two. Player Two has to control and pass quickly to another player in the circle, before Player One prevents the pass.

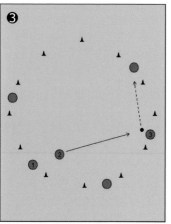

❸ Player Two then follows the pass, to put pressure on Player Three. This time, Player Three has to control and pass quickly to another player in the circle, before Player Two prevents the pass. Player One takes the place of Player Two in the circle, to be available for another pass.

Possible changes

■ Play as passive pressure, or players being fully committed to preventing the pass.
■ First touch passes only.

HOLD UP

How it works

❶ Players stand evenly spaced around the circle. The red player in the centre of the circle starts by making a move towards another red player, on the outside of the circle.

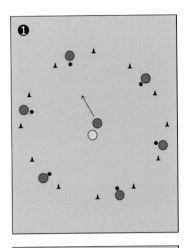

❷ The yellow defender stays close to the red player, to apply pressure. The red player receives a pass from the player on the outside of the circle.

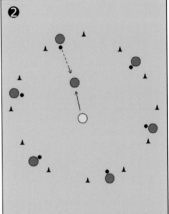

❸ The red player passes the ball back to the outside, and then moves quickly away to repeat this sequence, with another player, on the outside of the circle. The yellow player can be a passive defender at first, (just applying pressure), and can then become more active, (trying to win the ball), dependent on ability.

Possible changes

Half the players on the outside of the circle have a ball. This time the red player in the middle has to receive a pass and hold up the ball, whilst holding off the defender. They then pass to a different player on the outside of the circle, who doesn't already have a ball.

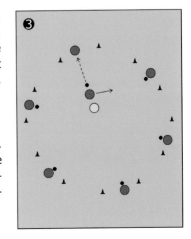

ONE-TWO PASSING

How it works

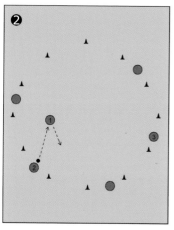

❶ Players stand evenly spaced around the circle. Player One starts by passing the ball to any other player in the circle, in this case Player Two.

❷ Player One then follows the pass towards Player Two. Player Two has to control and pass back to Player One, who then lays the ball off for Player Two to pass to another red player.

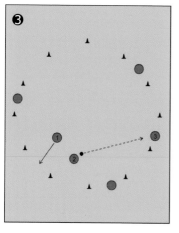

❸ Player Two then follows the pass, to perform a one-two with Player Three. Player one takes the place of Player Two in the circle, to be available for another pass.

Possible changes

■ First touch passes only.

ON YOUR TOES

How it works

❶ The yellow players in the centre of the circle start by passing the ball to any red player, around the outside of the playing area.

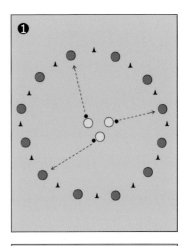

❷ The red player receiving a ball, then passes to another player who is next to them, on the outside of the circle. Yellow players move towards the outside of the circle, ready to receive a pass.

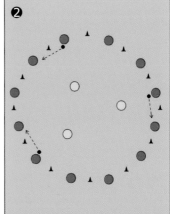

❸ The red player passes back to the yellow player inside the circle, who then moves off and repeats this passing combination somewhere else around the circle.

Possible changes

■ The red player who receives the first pass, can then pass to any other player around the circle. The yellow player has to follow the line of their pass, to be ready to receive a return pass.

■ Reduce or increase the number of players inside, or around the edge of the circle, dependent on ability.

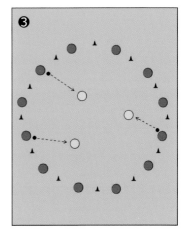

ONE-TWO AND THREE

How it works

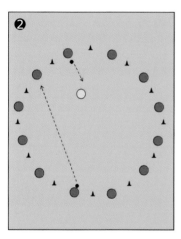

❶ The yellow player in the centre of the circle, starts by passing the ball to any red player around the outside of the circular playing area. At the same time, a red player with a ball on the outside of the circle, passes to any other available red player.

❷ The yellow player then follows their pass, to receive the ball back from the red player on the outside of the circle. The other red player continues to pass the ball to another player, around the edge of the playing area.

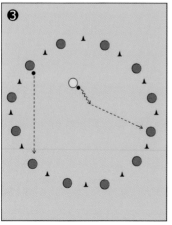

❸ This continues with one ball being passed, just between the outer players, while the other ball is passed back into the middle player, and then to the outside. Challenge the group to continue this sequence for one or two minutes, without any errors. Swap the yellow player after a few attempts, or when an outer player makes a mistake.

Possible changes

- Add another yellow player into the middle of the circle, or an extra ball passed around the outside, or both, dependent on ability.

CHAPTER 4

Single Grid Drills

Many of the practises contained within this chapter are designed to introduce, rehearse and refine the many passing, receiving, turning and dribbling techniques required to play, and enjoy, this beautiful game. Developing techniques is an important aspect for all players, young or old. They may be taught in isolation to begin with, allowing players time to correct faults and improve at their own pace, but once the basics have been grasped, they need to be practised as part of a variety of game-type activities. The ultimate aim, after all, is for players to perform these techniques with control and accuracy, within the pressures of a full game situation. The word 'instinctive' comes to mind, with quality players automatically knowing which technique to use, without even having to think.

To get to this stage, however, takes a lot of work and effort on behalf of both the coach and the player. It is vital that the coach creates both a sense of enjoyment, and challenge, within such practises, rather than just allowing for long periods of mundane repetition. These drills are designed for players to rehearse these techniques, whilst combining them with movement, both in possession and, just as importantly, when not in possession of the ball. This should help players when they come to transfer these techniques into game play.

You could also try challenging your players to achieve an individual skill target for players to try and achieve for the next ses-

sion with, of course, something in mind to reward their efforts. Yet, it is also up to the players themselves to have the dedication to practise these techniques at every opportunity, if they are to achieve their full potential; whether it be kicking a ball up against a wall, or playing with family or friends out in the back garden. Any opportunities to practise with a ball at their feet should be actively encouraged.

POSSIBLE SESSIONS

The following selections are only suggestions of how drills could be combined to create a one, or two-hour session. As a teacher, or coach, you need to assess the ability of your group and take into account possible numbers, before making appropriate choices of your own. All these sessions could also be started with a warm-up of your own and ended with some regular, small-sided games.

- The Chase
- Eye of the Needle
- Gridlock

- Cone Running
- Fill the Space
- W Passing
- Criss Cross
- Middle Pair

- Pass versus Dribble
- Spare Player Passing
- Horseshoes

- First Touch Square
- Pass and Follow
- Clock Passing
- Middle Mover
- Fourball

THE CHASE

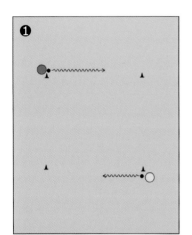

How it works

❶ Two players start with a ball each, at opposite corners of the grid. On a signal from the coach, both players must dribble their ball around the outside of the grid, in the same direction.

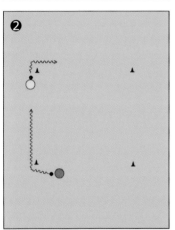

❷ The Chase lasts from thirty seconds up to one minute. Can either of the players catch each other within that time limit? Score as follows and then swap partners before playing again:

- five points for a catch;
- three points for being less than one cone-length from the other player;
- one point for being closer than the two-cone starting distance to the other player.

You could play a knockout competition if you wanted to end up with a 'Champion Chaser'.

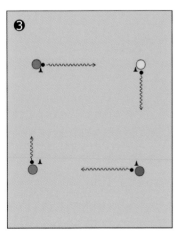

❸ **Possible changes**

- Play without dribbling the ball, as a straightforward running chase, or have the Chaser start only one cone-length behind the player they are chasing.
- Both players in the chase must dribble the ball a full circle around each corner cone, or perform another skill, before dribbling to the next cone.
- The Chaser, (without a ball), starts one cone-length ahead of the other player, (dribbling a ball). How long, (or how many cones can the player get round), before the Chaser catches them?
- Play a knockout game, (as shown in the diagram), with four players who are all trying to catch the player ahead of them. If a player is caught, they must drop out of the competition.

CAT AND MOUSE

How it works

❶ Two players start with a ball each, at opposite corners of the grid. Both players must dribble their ball, but must stay inside the grid at all times.

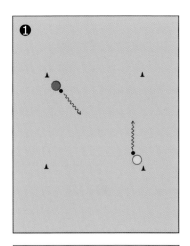

❷ The red player must try to tag the yellow player, whilst dribbling the ball under control. The yellow player must avoid being tagged, whilst dribbling the ball under control. If the yellow player is tagged, both players must return to opposite corners of the grid, before starting again. If the yellow player loses control of the ball out of the grid, then it counts as a tag and players restart at opposite corners as before.

   Play for one minute, or three or four attempts, and then the yellow player becomes the chaser. Play for two or three rounds and then change partners, putting players who got the most/least tags against each other.

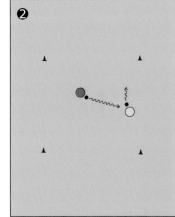

❸ **Possible changes**
   ▪ Play a knockout game with four players, who are allowed to tag any other player. If a player is tagged, or loses control of the ball, they drop out of the competition.

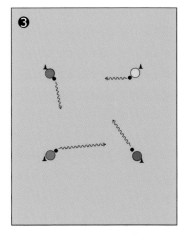

EYE OF THE NEEDLE

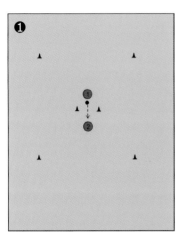

How it works

❶ Players One and Two stand opposite each other, at either side of a cone gate, in the centre of a grid. Both players pass the ball to each other through the 'eye of the needle', (cone gate).

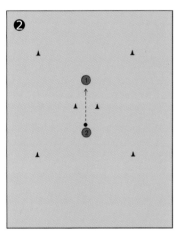

❷ After five or ten passes, both red players take a step backwards and repeat. If a mistake is made, (the ball not going through the gate, or not stopping the ball under control), then the players have to take a step in, closer to the cones.

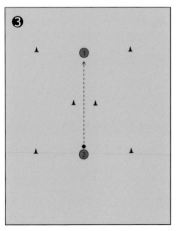

❸ The challenge is for the players to get to the edge of the grid and complete the set number of passes from there.

Possible changes

■ Limit to just one controlling touch before the pass, or first time passing only, depending on the ability of the players.

EYE OF THE NEEDLE 2

How it works
❶ Player One stands opposite Player Two, as shown in this diagram. Player Two passes the ball to Player One.

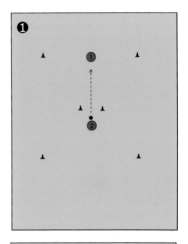

❷ Player One controls the ball, whilst Player Two runs to the end of the grid, turns and runs back towards the cone gate.

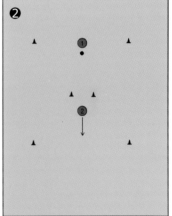

❸ As Player Two runs towards the middle, Player One times the pass to get to them just as they arrive at the cone gate. Player Two can take a touch, or pass the ball first time. The challenge is to complete five or ten passes without mistakes. Then swap player roles and repeat.

Possible changes
■ Player One picks up the ball and feeds in the air for a side-foot volley, header, or control and pass from Player Two.
■ Players could run backwards to the edge of the grid, and then forwards to the gate.

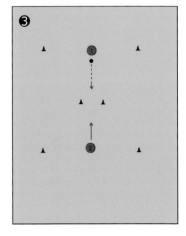

FIRST TOUCH SQUARE

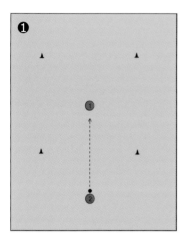

How it works

❶ Player One stands in the middle of a grid. Each cone is given a number, one to four, or the name of a soccer team. Player Two passes the ball in to Player One, at the same time as calling out a number, or the name of a cone.

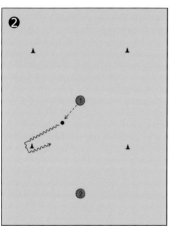

❷ Player One has to react to the call, by playing their first touch towards that cone. They then continue to dribble the ball around the cone, to return to the middle of the grid.

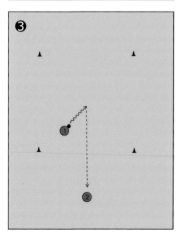

❸ Then Player One turns and passes back to Player Two. Player Two then repeats the pass, calling a different cone number/name each time. Reverse player roles after ten or twenty attempts.

Possible changes

■ Player Two can feed the ball in the air for Player One to control with their knee, or chest towards the named cone.

■ Player Two calls the number or name of the cone, before passing the ball, to give Player One more time to think about where to play their first touch.

RUNNING DIAGONALS

How it works

❶ Player One dribbles with the ball, diagonally across the grid.

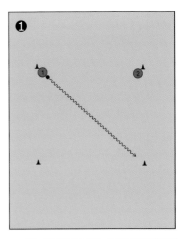

❷ Player One turns and passes to Player Two.

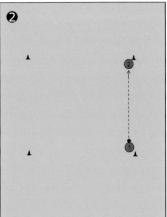

❸ Player Two dribbles with the ball, diagonally across the grid and then turns at the cone to pass to Player One. The drill continues with this dribbling and passing sequence.

Challenge the players to keep this passing sequence going, with no errors, for thirty seconds or one minute. Which group can keep going the longest without an error?

Possible changes

■ Reverse the direction of the drill, so that Player Two starts with the ball, (see first diagram), and players turn in a different direction.

■ Two pairs of players can perform this drill in the same grid, at the same time, starting at opposite ends.

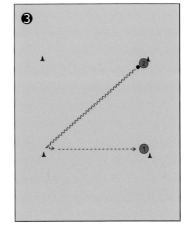

OPPOSITE CORNERS

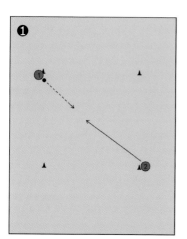

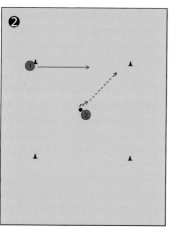

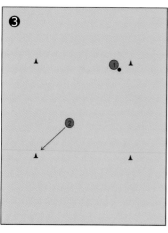

How it works

❶ Each player starts at opposite corners of a grid. Player Two makes a run to the centre of the grid. Player One passes the ball in to the feet of Player Two.

❷ Player One then makes a move to either of the cones, to each side of them. Player Two makes a turn to respond to the direction of Player One, and passes to the cone towards which the player is running.

❸ Player One runs on to receive and control the ball at the cone. Player Two must then run to the opposite corner, ready to repeat the drill. Reverse the player roles after one or two minutes, or until ten passing sequences have been completed. Can the players keep the drill going for thirty seconds or one minute without errors? Which group can keep going the longest without an error?

Possible changes

■ For advanced players, try four players repeating the same drill in the same grid. Players need to be aware of each other, especially when crossing in the middle of the grid. Limit the players to always moving and passing clockwise or, if they really want a challenge, let them move freely to one side or the other.

CONE RUNNING

How it works

❶ Three players stand in a grid, one with a ball. Player One passes the ball to Player Two, and then starts to make a run around a corner cone.

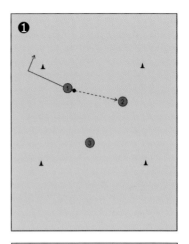

❷ Player Two passes to Player Three and then also starts to make a run around a corner cone. Player One continues their run around a corner cone, to get back into the grid.

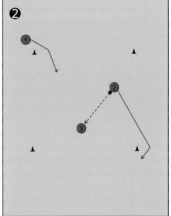

❸ Player Three passes to Player One, and starts to make a run around a corner cone. Player Two continues their run to get back into the grid for a pass from Player One. The drill continues with this repeated passing and moving sequence. Challenge the players to keep the passing sequence going with no errors for thirty seconds or one minute. Which group can keep going the longest without an error?

Possible changes

- First touch passes only.
- Have two groups of three, working separately in the same grid at the same time – this really tests them!

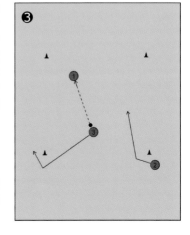

FILL THE SPACE

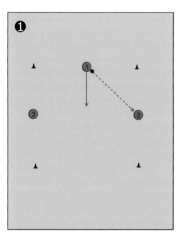

How it works

❶ Three players stand half way between the cones on the sides of the grid. Player One passes the ball to Player Two, and then runs to fill the space on the empty side of the grid.

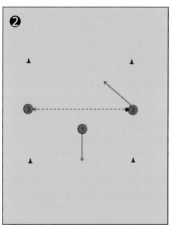

❷ Player Two passes the ball to Player Three, and then makes a run to fill in the space on the empty side of the grid. Player One completes their run across the grid and turns, ready to receive a pass.

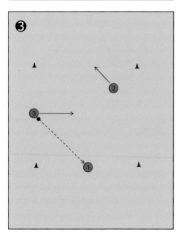

❸ Player Three passes the ball to Player One, and then makes a run to fill the space on the empty side of the grid. The drill continues with this repeated passing and moving sequence. Challenge players to keep the passing sequence going with no errors for thirty seconds or one minute. Which group can keep going the longest without an error?

Possible changes

■ First touch passes only.

DIAGONALS

How it works
❶ Three players stand by a cone in a different corner of the grid, one of them with a ball. Player One dribbles with the ball to the spare cone.

❷ Player One turns at the cone and passes diagonally across the grid to Player Two.

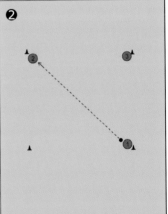

❸ Player Two dribbles with the ball to the spare cone, and then turns to pass diagonally across the grid to Player Three. Player Three then dribbles to the spare cone, and passes diagonally across the grid to Player One. The drill continues with this repeated passing and moving sequence. Challenge the players to keep the passing sequence going with no errors for thirty seconds or one minute. Which group can keep going the longest without an error?

Possible changes
■ Reverse the direction of the drill so that Player Three starts with the ball, (see first diagram), and the players are moving and turning in a different direction.

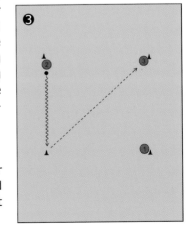

HORSESHOES

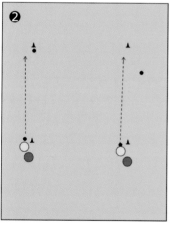

How it works

❶ Two players stand together at the corners of a grid, as shown in this diagram.

   The red player passes the ball, to get it as close to the other cone as possible.

❷ The yellow player then passes their ball to try and get closer to the cone, in order to score a point. If either player gets their ball to stop right next to the cone, (a toucher), it counts as three points.

❸ The yellow player can play to knock the other ball away in an attempt to get closer, or to prevent the red player from scoring three points for a toucher. The player who scores the point goes first each time, or they can just take it in turns. Winners and losers could then move on to play each other in a competition.

Possible changes

■ Mark an area around the target cone to count as a scoring zone. The ball must be inside this area to score a point.

■ Use two balls each, if you have a good supply.

■ Lengthen the distance between the cones, depending upon the ability of your group, or even each pair within your group.

■ Award the players five points for knocking the cone over.

PASS VERSUS DRIBBLE

How it works

❶ Four players stand at different corners of the grid, as shown in the diagram. On a signal from the coach, the red players start to pass the ball between each other. Meanwhile, the yellow players have to dribble the ball out towards the opposite cone.

❷ The red players continue to pass the ball between each other as fast as they can, without losing control. (You can get them to shout out the numbers as they count). The yellow player has to touch the cone, and then dribble back to stop the ball at their partner's feet.

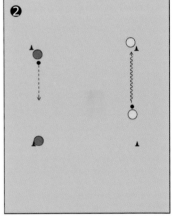

❸ The yellow players have to complete five dribbles each and then shout: 'Stop'. At this point the red players have to stop passing. How many passes were the red players able to complete in this time? Swap over and the yellow team has to try and beat the number of passes set by the reds.

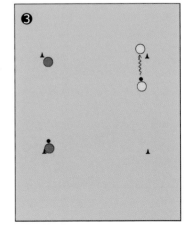

Possible changes

■ Players dribble out to touch the opposite cone, but are then allowed to pass the ball back.

■ Set a one-minute time limit for both pairs. Challenge them to beat previous records, set by different pairs.

■ First touch passes only.

SPARE PLAYER PASSING

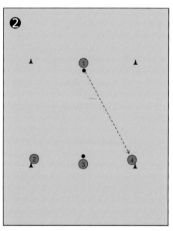

How it works

❶ Three players at one end of the grid, two with balls, face one player at the opposite side of the grid. Player Two passes the ball to Player One.

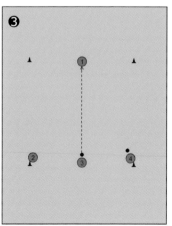

❷ Player One passes to Player Four.

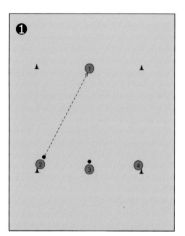

❸ Player Three passes to Player One, who then passes to Player Two. The practise carries on with Player One passing to the spare player without a ball, and continues with this repeated passing sequence. Challenge the players to keep the passing sequence going with no errors for thirty seconds or one minute. Which group can keep going the longest without an error?

Possible changes
- Controlling touch with one foot, pass with the other.
- First touch passes only.
- Player One has to make a run around one of the cones at their end of the grid, between passes.

GRIDLOCK

How it works

❶ Red player One starts by passing the ball to Yellow Player One, and then runs around either cone at their end of the grid.

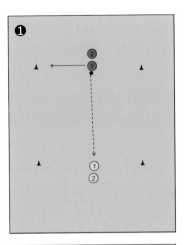

❷ Yellow Player One controls the ball and passes it back to Red Player Two. Yellow Player One then runs around either cone at their end of the grid. The pass and move sequence continues with Red Player Two passing to Yellow Player Two, and so on.

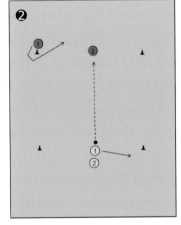

❸ On a signal from the coach, this passing sequence stops and a two versus two game begins, with the team in possession of the ball becoming the attackers. The yellow team scores by passing the ball to knock over either of the cones at the opposite end of the grid, (break the gridlock). The red team attempt to prevent this from happening, or try to win possession of the ball for them to score. The game is over as soon as the ball leaves the grid. When all groups have finished, start them all with the passing sequence again for another game.

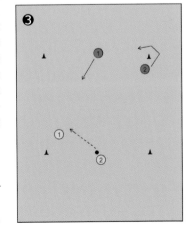

Possible changes

■ A player must stop the ball anywhere in line between the two cones, in order to score a point.
■ First touch passes only during the opening sequence.

PASS AND FOLLOW

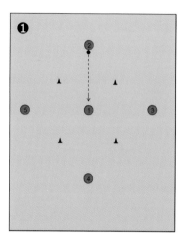

How it works

❶ One player stands in the grid, with four more players standing around the outside, one having a ball. Player Two passes the ball into the grid to Player One.

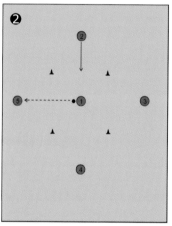

❷ Player Two follows their pass and takes up a position in the middle of the grid. Player One turns and passes the ball out to any of the other players around the grid, in this case Player Five.

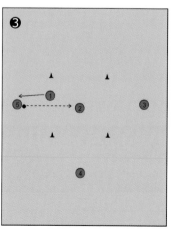

❸ Player Five passes the ball to Player Two who must turn and pass the ball out of the grid to either Player Three or Four. The drill continues with this repeated passing and moving sequence. Challenge the players to keep the passing sequence going with no errors for thirty seconds or one minute. Which group can keep going the longest without an error?

Possible changes

■ Players could start by just dribbling the ball in this sequence, to get used to the movement required. Then the player in the centre could dribble the ball out of the grid, to stop it for the next player to make the pass back in. Continue this dribble out and pass in sequence.

CLOCK PASSING

How it works

❶ One player stands in the grid, with four more players standing around the outside, each having a ball. Players on the outside of the grid are given the numbers corresponding to quarter hours of the clock: three, six, nine and twelve. Player One has to call out the numbers of the other players. In this diagram, Player One has called the number six. Player One makes a run towards that player, up to the edge of the grid. Player Six then passes the ball to Player One.

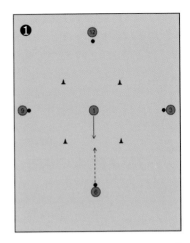

❷ Player One passes back to Player Six and returns to the centre of the grid.

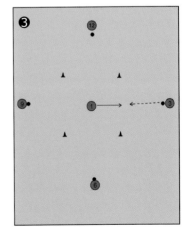

❷ Player One calls another number, in this case three. Player One makes a run towards that player, up to the edge of the grid. Player Three then passes the ball to Player One, who plays it back and returns to the centre of the grid. The drill continues with this repeated passing and moving sequence. Challenge the players to keep this passing sequence going, with no errors, for thirty seconds or one minute. Which group can keep going the longest without an error?

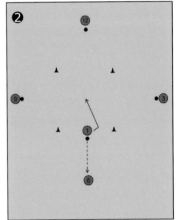

Possible changes

■ The coach, or an outside player, calls the numbers. Use North, South, East and West, or numbers one to four, if you prefer.
■ First touch passes only.
■ Play in a circle with all, or most, of the hours of the clock and two, or even three, players in the middle, calling their own times.

BEAT THE CONE

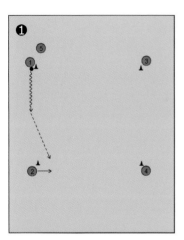

How it works

❶ Player One begins by dribbling the ball towards Player Two. Player One then passes the ball in front of the cone, for Player Two to run on to receive.

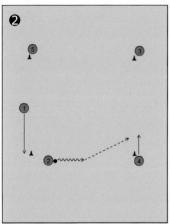

❷ Player Two controls the ball, continues to dribble and then passes in front of the cone to Player Four. Player One continues their run until they reach the corner cone.

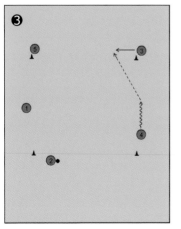

❸ The ball is passed around the grid in a similar pattern. Challenge the players to maintain fluency with no mistakes for one minute, or time how many passes they can make in that time period.

Possible changes

■ Make it one touch to control the ball in front of them, and one touch to pass to the next player.

BEAT THE CONE 2

How it works

❶ Player One begins by dribbling the ball towards Player Two, who makes a move towards Player One to receive a pass.

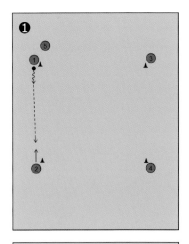

❷ Player Two passes the ball back to Player One, and then turns to make a run around the corner cone of the grid.

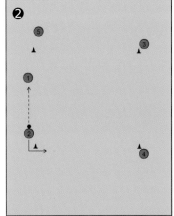

❸ Player One completes the sequence by passing back to Player Two. Player Four then makes a move towards Player Two, ready to receive the next pass. Player Two then repeats the same sequence of passes with Player Four, and the ball continues around the grid in the same way. Meanwhile Player One continues their run until they reach the corner cone.

Challenge the players to maintain fluency with no mistakes for one or two minutes, or time how many passes they can make in that time period.

Possible changes

■ Make it one touch to control the ball in front of the players, and one touch to pass to the next player.

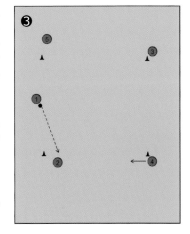

FOUR BALL

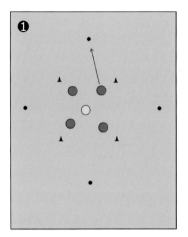

How it works

❶ A red player runs out of the grid to collect a ball. This player must pass the ball into the grid to another red player, and then join them to help keep possession of the ball. The yellow player acts as a defender, and tries to tackle or intercept the ball.

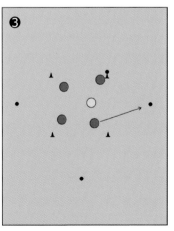

❷ The red players try to complete a set number of passes, such as ten. If the yellow player gains possession of the ball and kicks it out of the grid, then that ball is lost. A different red player then has to run out of the grid to get another ball, in order to start the set number of passes again.

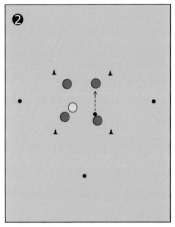

❸ If ten passes are completed, a red player can dribble the ball to a corner cone and place it on top. A different red player then runs out of the grid to collect another ball, and the possession game is repeated. The red players have to try to get all four balls on top of the cones to win the game outright. However, the yellow player can win the game outright by gaining possession of a ball and passing it to knock another ball off a corner cone. If this is achieved, the game stops.

Possible changes

■ This can be played three versus one, five versus one, five versus two, or any combination of numbers, just alter the size of the grid accordingly.

■ Set a stopwatch and create a record time for different teams to try and beat.

MIDDLE MOVER

How it works

❶ Four players stand by a cone in each corner of the grid, one with a ball, with another player standing in the middle. Player One passes the ball to the middle player.

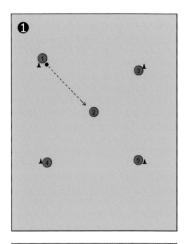

❷ Player One then follows their pass to the middle, whilst Player Two turns and passes to any other player at the corner of a grid.

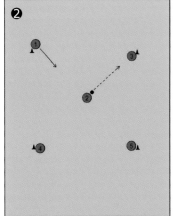

❸ Player Three then passes the ball to Player One, who is now in the middle of the grid. Player Two fills the space in the empty corner of the grid. Player Three then follows their pass to the middle, whilst Player One turns and passes to any other player at the corner of the grid. Player One then fills the space in the empty corner of the grid. Challenge the players to keep going for a set amount of time without errors, or see how quickly they can make twenty or thirty passes.

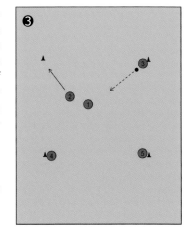

Possible changes

■ Get the players to dribble and stop the ball first, to get used to the pattern of movement.

MIDDLE PAIR

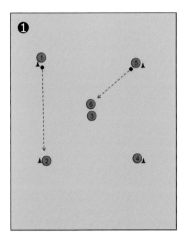

How it works

❶ Four players stand by a cone in each corner of the grid, two with a ball, with another two players standing in the middle. Players can pass the ball to any other player who is available to receive the ball.

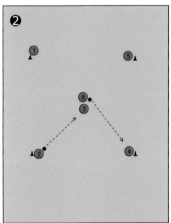

❷ The middle players are not allowed to pass to each other, but any other passes are allowed. Challenge the group to continue for one or two minutes without an error, or time how long it takes for the group to complete twenty or thirty passes.

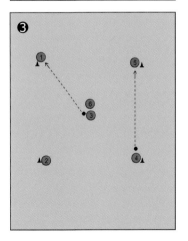

❸ **Possible changes**

■ Use one ball first, to familiarize players with the drill.

■ First touch passes only.

■ Get the players to follow their passes with two balls going, if you really want a challenge!

W PASSING

How it works

❶ Five players stand by a cone in each corner of the grid, one with a ball, with another player standing in the middle. Player One passes the ball to Player Two and then follows the pass.

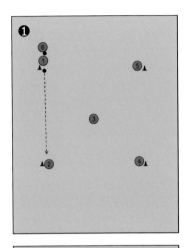

❷ Player Two has one touch to control the ball, and then passes to Player Three in the middle of the grid. Player Two follows their pass.

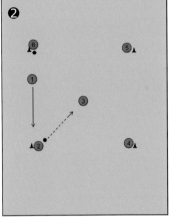

❸ Player Three has one touch to control the ball and then passes to Player Four. Player Three then follows their pass. As soon as Player One has reached the cone, Player Six can start another ball. Players continue to pass and follow until the ball gets to Player Five, who dribbles the ball across to the starting point, ready to pass. Challenge the group to continue for one or two minutes without an error, or time how long it takes for everyone in the group to get back to their starting positions and then try to beat it.

Possible changes

■ Dribble with the ball first, to get used to the pattern of movement.

■ First touch passes only.

■ Just use one ball and have Player Five pass to Player Six to start the sequence of pass and follow again.

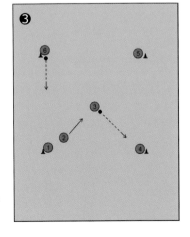

CRISS CROSS

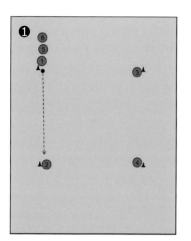

How it works

❶ Four players stand by a cone in each corner of the grid, one with a ball, with other players standing behind Player One. Player One passes the ball to Player Two, and then follows the pass.

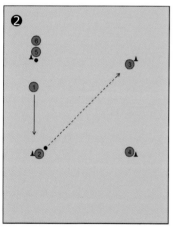

❷ Player Two has one touch to control the ball, and then passes diagonally across the grid to Player Three. Player Two follows their pass.

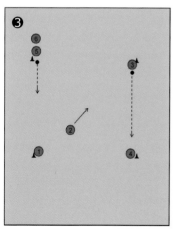

❸ Player Three has one touch to control the ball, and then passes to Player Four. Player Three follows their pass. As soon as Player One has reached the cone, Player Five can start another ball. Player Four has one touch to control and pass the ball, diagonally across the grid to Player Six. Players continue to pass and follow in this sequence. Take care to time passes and runs diagonally, across the grid. Challenge the group to continue for one or two minutes without an error, or time how long it takes for all of the group to get back to their starting positions and then try to beat it.

Possible changes

■ Dribble with the ball first to get used to the pattern of movement.
■ First touch passes only.

CROSSFIRE

How it works

❶ Player Ones pass the ball across the grid to Player Twos.

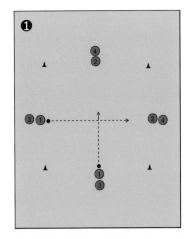

❷ Player Ones then make a move to their right, to join a new line.

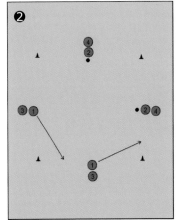

❸ Player Twos pass the ball back across the grid to Player Threes and then move to their right to join a new line. Challenge the players to keep this passing sequence going for thirty seconds or one minute, without a collision of balls, or any other errors.

Possible changes

■ Players follow their pass across the grid to join the line at the opposite side of the grid – watch out!

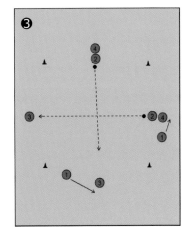

PASS AND MOVE

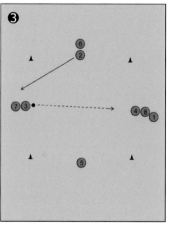

How it works

❶ Two players start in the middle of each side of a grid. Player One starts by passing the ball to Player Two.

❷ Player One then makes a diagonal run to the right, to join the line. Player Two passes to Player Three.

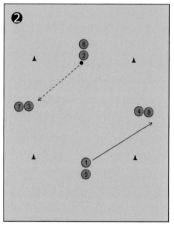

❸ Player Two then makes the run, whilst Player Three passes across the grid to Player Four. The passing and moving sequence continues with Player Four passing to Player Five and so on. Challenge the players to see how long they can continue without errors, or set a target number of passes to make within a set amount of time.

Possible changes

■ Reverse the passing and moving sequence to the left.

■ First touch passes only.

■ Add another player at each side of the grid. Repeat the same passing and moving sequence, but have both Player One and Player Three start with a ball.

CHAPTER 5

Multiple Grid and Channel Drills

After setting up a series of adjacent individual grids, these drills provide an almost seamless progression into using a large area of combined grids, or the long narrow channels created by them. Many of the drills in this section can, therefore, be used in conjunction with those from the previous chapter, to provide the next step, or extra group challenge, for developing techniques in more game-type activities.

It is one thing to practise and master specific skills, but quite another to have the ability to use these to good effect in the pressure of these game situations. Using passive defenders is an important step in allowing your players to experience this pressure from opponents, whilst giving them the opportunity to become confident in their own ability to perform these skills consistently. This is because passive defenders are only allowed to get close to players, without actually trying to win possession by making tackles. You can also decide whether or not to allow them to intercept passes between players. Make them fully active too soon, and the practise will continually break down and player

confidence may be dented. Delay for too long and players may not receive the level of challenge they need to make progress.

POSSIBLE SESSIONS

The following selections are only suggestions of how drills could be combined to create a one, or two-hour session. As a teacher, or coach, you need to assess the ability of your group and take into account possible numbers, before making appropriate choices of your own. All these sessions could also be started with a warm-up of your own, and ended with some regular, small-sided games.

- Pizza Party Relay
- Ten Pin Bowling
- Gladiators

- Cone Numbers
- No Man's Land
- Goalie Swap

- Quick Touches
- Hit and Run
- Line Drill
- Squareball
- Through the Centre

- Bombs Away 2
- Passing Combo
- Grid Race
- Knock Off
- Head for Goal

ONE VERSUS ONE CONE GATES

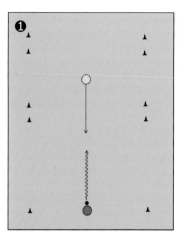

How it works

❶ The red player, (attacker), moves forward with the ball in an attempt to try and dribble it through one of the four cone gates. The yellow player, (defender), moves forward to prevent the red player from doing so.

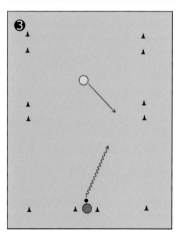

❷ The red player scores one point for dribbling the ball through one of the nearer gates, and three points if they go through one of the further gates. The yellow defender tries to win the ball in a tackle, or pressure the opponent to make them move away from the gate, or lose control. If this happens, both players must return to their start positions. Play five times, then swap roles. Play for two or three rounds and then change partners, putting players who got the most/least points against each other.

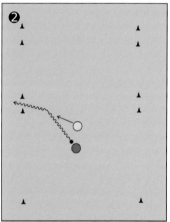

❸ **Possible changes**

■ If the yellow player wins the ball, they can score three points by passing, or dribbling, the ball through the cone gate at the red player's end of the playing area.

■ Play keeps going until one of the players score a point(s), or the ball leaves the playing area, in which case both players return to their starting positions and begin again.

■ You could also play two versus one, or two versus two.

HEAD FOR GOAL

How it works

❶ Red Player One starts the drill, by throwing the ball up for Red Player Two. Red Player Two must head the ball from within their grid.

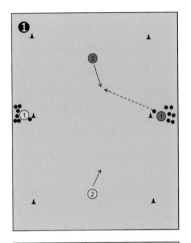

❷ Red Player Two heads for goal, to score between the cones at the opposite end of the channel. A goal must be below head height of Player Two, who is in goal at the time. You can allow goalkeepers to use their hands, or not, as you prefer.

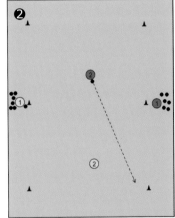

❸ As soon as a goal has been scored, or Yellow Player Two has made a save, Yellow Player One throws the ball up for their partner to run on to, and try to score in the red goal. If the throw from Yellow Player One is not good enough for Yellow Player Two to attempt a header, then they don't get another turn. The red team can make an attempt on goal as soon as they are ready. Each Player One needs a few balls to keep the game flowing. The first team to five goals is the winner. Then change the roles of the players. You could play a knockout, or round-robin tournament, if you have a larger group.

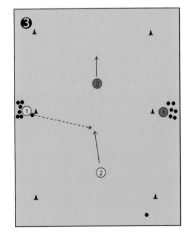

Possible changes

■ Allow both players from each team inside their own grid. They are allowed to throw to each other, and either of them can head for goal and both can act as goalkeepers.

■ Reduce the size of the grid for younger players.

PASSING COMBO

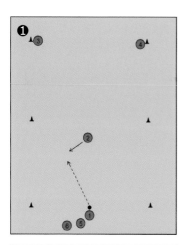

How it works

❶ This drill takes place in two adjacent grids. Player One starts the drill by passing the ball to either side of Player Two.

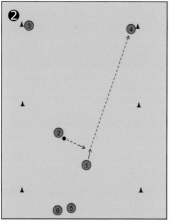

❷ Player Two then passes the ball, ahead of Player One, for them to run on to. Player One then passes to Player Four, and follows the pass to take that place.

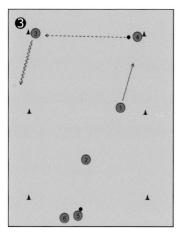

❸ Player Four then passes to Player Three, and Player Four follows the pass to take that place. Player Three dribbles the ball back up to the starting point and joins the end of the line. Player Five repeats the drill by passing to either side of Player Two, as soon as Player One has reached the far corner cone. Change Player Two after a few repetitions.

Possible changes

■ Player Two picks up the ball and feeds it to the other players, for them to control on the move and then pass.

PASSING COMBO 2

How it works

❶ This drill takes place in two adjacent grids. Player One starts the drill by passing the ball to Player Four. Player One follows this pass around the cones at the side of the channel.

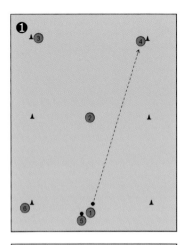

❷ Player Four controls the ball and passes to Player Two. Player Two then passes to Player Three, and all the players continue to follow their passes.

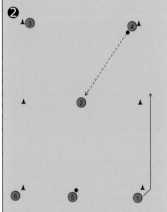

❸ Player Three then passes down the side of the channel to Player Six. Players continue to follow their passes. Meanwhile, as soon as Player One has reached the far corner of the channel, Player Five starts the passing sequence again.

Possible changes

■ The two long passes must be lofted.

■ Player Four picks the ball up and feeds for Player Two to side-foot volley, or head the ball to Player Three.

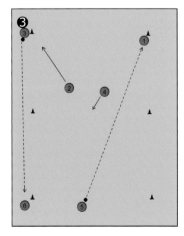

BOMBS AWAY 2

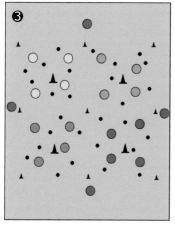

How it works

❶ This is a drill that I often use inside, as the balls will just bounce off the walls and back into play, but you can play it outside as well. Four teams start inside, next to adjacent squares with lots of balls, (bombs), spread around. A fifth team stands around the outside of the squares.

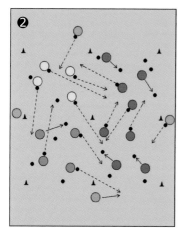

❷ On a signal from the coach, the players try to pass as many balls as they can into any of the other team's squares. The orange team and the coach can pass any balls back in that come out of the playing area. Play for one or two minutes, then stop and count up the number of balls, (bombs), in each square, to work out the winning team for that round. The team with the fewest balls in their grid is the winner. The orange team then swaps with one of the other teams and plays again. Then repeat, so that each team has been on the outside of the squares once. You could keep a running score at the end of each round to work out a final winning team.

❸ **Possible changes**

■ The players have to pick up a ball and feed it to one of their team-mates to head, or side-foot volley, into the opponent's playing area.

■ Place a large cone in the centre of each grid area. If a player hits the big cone of another team with a pass, they get one or two bombs knocked off their score at the end of the game.

KNOCK OFF

How it works

❶ The red players start with the ball, and have to keep possession from the yellow defender. The red players must stay in their own grid, but the yellow defender is allowed to move freely from one grid to another.

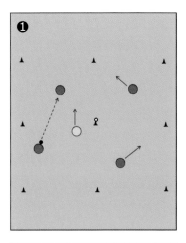

❷ The red players pass the ball between them, to try and create an opportunity to score.

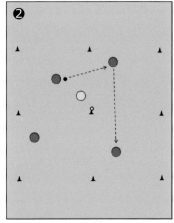

❸ The red team score by knocking the ball off the cone in the centre of the grids. If the red team score, the ball is replaced on top of the cone and play is restarted with a pass from a red player, at the edge of the playing area. If the yellow player intercepts the ball, or forces a mistake three times, then they swap with one of the red players.

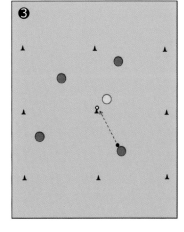

Possible changes

■ The red team have to complete ten passes, before they are allowed to try and knock the ball off the central cone.

■ Add a second yellow defender to make it more of a challenge, and/or another red player who is allowed to move freely between the grids.

GRID RACE

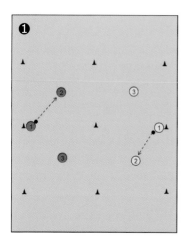

How it works

❶ Player Ones start by passing the ball to either of their two team-mates.

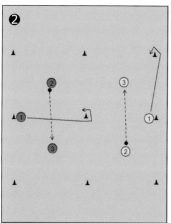

❷ After passing the ball, Player Ones must run around any cone in their two grids.

Player Twos pass the ball to Player Three.

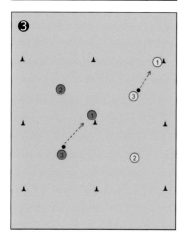

❸ As Player One comes around the cone, Player Three passes the ball in to their feet.

❹ Player Ones then pass straight back to Player Threes and run around another cone in the grid.

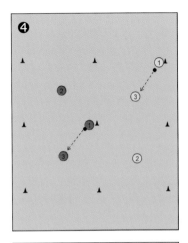

❺ Player Threes pass the ball across to Player Twos in the next grid.

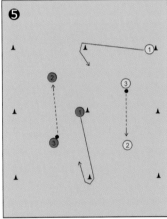

❻ Then as Player Ones run around the cone, they are passed the ball from Player Two, playing it back before, setting off for another cone. Teams compete against each other to get Player One around a target number of cones. Players then swap roles and race twice more, so that all players have taken each position.

Possible changes
■ To make it simpler, allow Player Ones to dribble the ball around a grid cone and then play a one-two with Player Two. They must then dribble the ball around a different cone and play a one-two with Player Three. Keep alternating cones and passes until the target number of cones has been achieved.

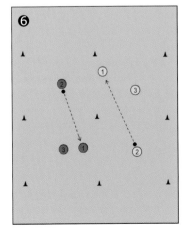

TEN PIN BOWLING

How it works

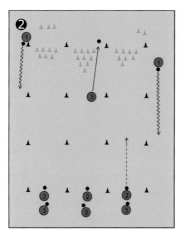

❶ A simple passing game, but you need a lot of tall cones that can be knocked over. Players in each team take it in turns to pass their ball down the channel, (bowling alley), to knock down as many cones, (pins), as possible.

❷ Each player must follow the pass to retrieve their ball, and can also move to the side any cones that have already been knocked down. As soon as Player One is out of the way, Player Two can pass at the cones.

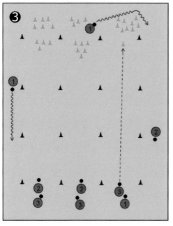

❸ The first team to knock down all of the cones wins, or the most number of cones knocked down after two or three passes for each player.

Possible changes

- Play it as a timed game, where the next player can pass as soon as the player before them is out of the way. Set a record to try and beat for the quickest time to knock down all the cones.
- Change the length of the channel, (bowling alley), to suit the ability of your players, or move the winning team a little further back for the next game.

TEN PIN BOWLING 2

How it works

❶ After playing Ten Pin Bowling you could try this for a bit of fun. This time the players are the pins, and each team takes it in turns to try and knock down all the pins in as few passes as possible.

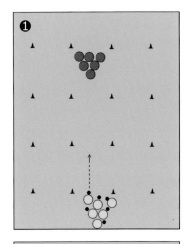

❷ Any red player the ball hits or touches, stands to the side. Players only get one pass each, to see how many of the other team they can 'knock down'.

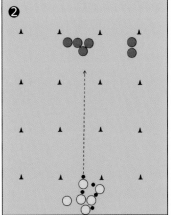

❸ Then the other team tries to beat their score. Passes must be sensibly paced, and below knee height for safety reasons.

Possible changes

■ Keep a running score, as in ten pin bowling, and the team with the best score after the set number of rounds is the winner.

PIZZA PARTY RELAY

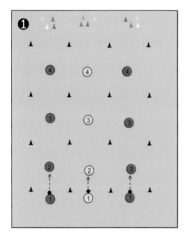

How it works

❶ Players line up in each grid of a channel, the first in each team having a ball at their feet. Placed at the far end of each channel are four different coloured cones. These are the toppings which have to be collected to finish making their pizza.

- Red – tomato
- Green – pepper
- White – mushroom
- Yellow – cheese

On a signal from the coach, the first player in each team passes the ball to Player Two.

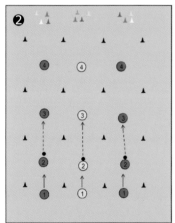

❷ Player Two then turns and passes to Player Three. Player One follows their pass and moves into the first grid of the channel.

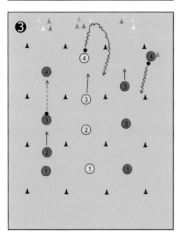

❸ Player Three then turns and passes to Player Four. Player Two follows their pass and moves into the second grid of the channel. Player Four then dribbles the ball to pick up a pizza topping, and back down to the start line at the other end of the channel to begin the passing sequence again. Player Three follows their pass and moves into the last grid of the channel. Players continue until Player One dribbles the ball and the last pizza topping down to the start.

Possible changes

- Players could dribble the ball and stop it at the next player's feet.
- Player One could have to dribble around a cone at the back of the first grid, before passing to Player Two, and so on for the other players down the grid.
- Place hoops at the start of each channel to act as the pizza dough, on which the players have to place the collected toppings.

CHANNEL RELAY

How it works

❶ Players line up in each grid of a channel, the first in each team having a ball at their feet. On a signal from the coach, the first player in each team passes the ball to Player Two. Player Two then passes back to Player One.

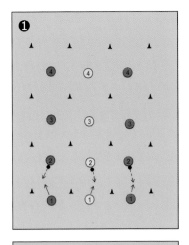

❷ Player One controls the ball and dribbles on to the next grid. Player One then passes to Player Three, receiving a pass straight back. Player One then continues to do the same with Player Four.

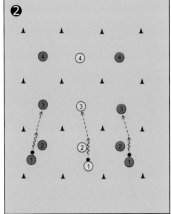

❸ When Player One receives the ball back from Player Four, they must dribble to the end of the channel, turn and pass to Player Four again. Player Four then turns and passes to Player Three, who does the same to Player Two. Player Two dribbles the ball to the start of the channel, turns and begins the passing sequence again. Players continue until Player One dribbles the ball back to the start line to finish the relay.

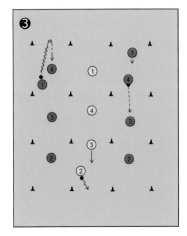

CHANNEL RELAY 2

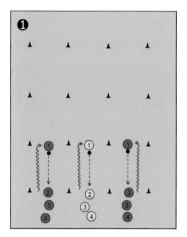

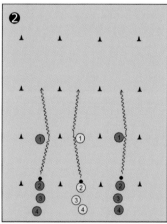

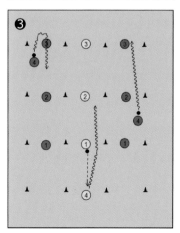

How it works

❶ Players line up at the end of a channel, the first in each team having a ball at their feet. On a signal from the coach, the first player in each team dribbles the ball to the end of the first grid. Player One then turns and passes back to Player Two.

❷ Player Two then dribbles the ball to the end of the second grid, turns and passes back to Player One, who turns and passes back to Player Three. Player Three then dribbles the ball to the end of the final grid in the channel, turns and passes to Player Two. Player Two controls the ball, turns and passes to Player One, who does the same and passes to Player Four.

❸ Player Four must then dribble the ball to the far end of the channel, turn and pass the ball through the legs of Player Three. Player Four then continues down the channel, passing the ball through the legs of each player as they go. As soon as the ball is passed through their legs, the other players are free to run back to the start line. The relay is finished when all the players are back at the start line. Repeat, but change the order of the players. The team who finished last/second, could then start the next relay with a slight time advantage over the team that finished first.

Possible changes

■ Players have to pass the ball between the legs of their team-mates and crawl through after it. Player Four then has to pass and crawl through all the legs of the other players, on their return to the start line.

TUNNELBALL RELAY

How it works

❶ Players line up at the end of a channel, the first in each team having a ball at their feet. On a signal from the coach, the first player in each team dribbles the ball to the end of the channel, turns and dribbles back towards the rest of their team. On the way back Player One must stop the ball between the cones, as shown in the diagram, and pass the ball to Player Two in their team.

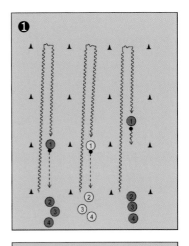

❷ Player Two must then dribble the ball to the end of the channel, turn and dribble back towards the rest of their team. Player One takes up a position, as shown in the diagram, with legs wide open.

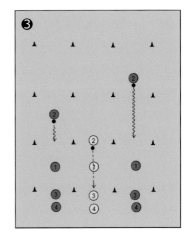

❸ Player Two stops the ball and then must pass through the legs of Player One, to get the ball to Player Three. If the pass does not get through Player One's legs, then the ball must be taken back and passed again. If the second pass does not get through, then Player Two can dribble the ball to Player Three. Player Three then dribbles to the end of the channel, whilst Player Two joins Player One, to make a two-player tunnel for Player Three to pass through. The relay ends when Player Four passes through a three-player tunnel, to get the ball past the start line.

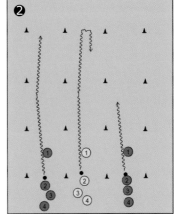

Possible changes

■ The players in the tunnel could help the ball through by using their hands, if other players are finding it difficult to pass accurately enough.

■ Have a ball balanced on top of a cone at each team's start line. If the ball goes through the tunnel and knocks the ball off the cone, that team instantly wins the relay, or gets five or ten seconds knocked off their time at the end.

CONE NUMBERS

How it works

❶ The coach numbers the corner cones of the grid, one to four. On a signal from the coach, Player Ones dribble into a grid at the start of a channel.

❷ As the players enter the grid, the coach calls a number. The players must dribble the ball around that cone, and then continue to the end of the channel. They then head back around the outside of the channels, to rejoin the end of their own line. The coach then repeats this for other players, calling different numbers each time.

❸ **Possible changes**

- Instead of numbers, use the names of famous, or local, soccer teams.
- As the players get used to the numbers, the coach can challenge players by calling two, three, or even four numbers at a time, in different combinations. Make sure that players keep their heads up whilst dribbling, so they are aware of others.

GOALIE SWAP

How it works

❶ Players stand at each end of a channel with a ball each. In the middle of the channel is a cone goal, with Player Five acting as a goalkeeper. Player One begins by dribbling the ball down the channel towards the goal.

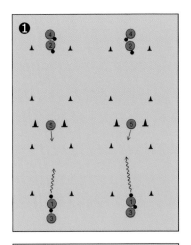

❷ Player One, in the channel on the left of the diagram, has decided to shoot to the corner of the goal. Player One, in the channel on the right of the diagram, has decided to dribble round the goalkeeper, before passing the ball into an empty goal.

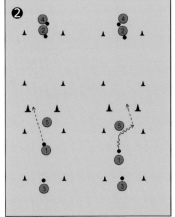

❸ Player One then takes the place of Player Five as the goalkeeper. Player Two then starts to dribble from the other end of the channel, to attempt to score on goal. Player Five retrieves the ball and dribbles down the sides of the channel to join Player Three. The players continue to rotate around in a similar way, so that all of them take on the role of the goalkeeper. After a few rounds you could make it more competitive by keeping score for each team, and also giving extra points for players demonstrating good skills.

Possible changes

■ Each player could start with three lives and lose one each time they fail to score, but also gain one if they made a good save as the goalkeeper.

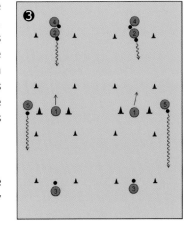

QUICK TOUCHES

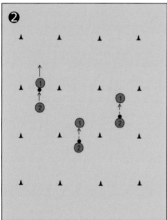

How it works

❶ Players One and Two stand facing each other, about two or three metres apart, at one end of the channel. Player Two starts by passing the ball to Player One. Player One stops the ball for Player Two to move forwards, and then jogs backwards to receive another pass.

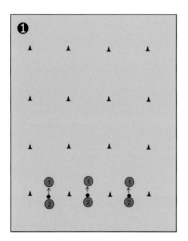

❷ Both players make their way down the channel using first-touch passes, Player One always moving backwards, with a light touch on the ball for Player Two to run on to. Players reverse roles and repeat the same sequence, moving back down the channel in the opposite direction.

Possible changes

■ Player Two holds the ball in their hands and feeds Player One, to return with a header or side-foot volley.
■ Players could throw the ball to each other first, as part of a warm-up.

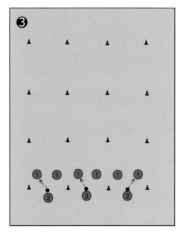

❸ Have two Player Ones and pass, or feed, to each player in turn as they move backwards down the channel.

LINE DRILL

How it works

❶ Player One and Two stand facing each other, at opposite ends of the first grid, in a longer channel. Player Two starts by feeding the ball for Player One to return with a header. Repeat ten times.

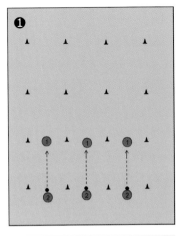

❷ Player One then moves back to the next line of cones. Player Two performs a throw-in for Player One to get in line, control the ball, and then pass back to Player Two. Repeat ten times.

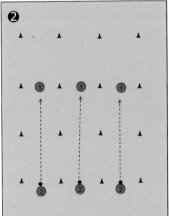

❸ Player One then moves back to the end line of cones. Players One and Two then have to complete twenty lofted passes to each other. Players then reverse roles and repeat.

Possible changes

■ Vary the skills performed at each line of cones, such as short, first-touch passes, feed the ball for a side-foot volley, roll the ball for a chipped return, and so on.

■ Give a signal for all players to move back to the next cone at the same time.

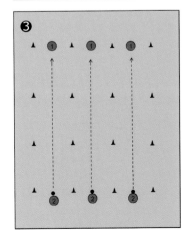

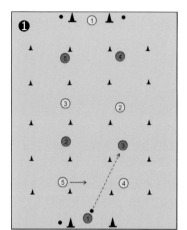

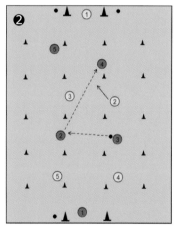

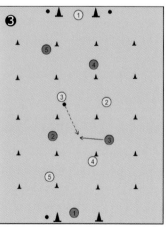

SNAKES AND LADDERS

How it works

❶ Red Player One starts the game by trying to pass through the yellow zone of the ladder, to either of the red players. As the red team has possession of the ball, the yellow players become the snakes in the game. In this diagram, the ball has been passed to Red Player Three. That player has to control the ball inside that zone, and then combine with Red Player Two to try and pass through the next yellow snakes to Red Players Four or Five. All the players must stay within their own zones of the ladder. Have some spare balls next to each goal, so that play can be restarted quickly.

❷ The ball has successfully reached the red players in the last zone of the ladder. They can pass between each other, to create a shooting opportunity from within that zone and try to score past Yellow Player One. Score or miss, Yellow Player One gets another ball and starts the game in the opposite direction, by trying to pass through the red zone to Yellow Players Two or Three and so on, to try and score. This time the red players become the snakes, to try and prevent the yellow team scoring a goal.

❸ In this diagram Red Player Three, (snake), has intercepted a pass through their zone. They can, therefore, try and pass through to Red Players Four or Five to try and score. If a ball is lost outside the playing area, then the team who were not in possession, restart the game with a pass in from Player One. Change players around into different zones after a while and continue, or start another game.

Possible changes

■ Allow lofted passes between zones, such as from Player One to Player Four.

■ Player One, acting as the goalkeeper, can throw the ball directly into either of the two zones occupied by their team.

■ Allow each team to start a ball at the same time, and then keep two balls in play.

GLADIATORS

How it works

❶ Teams of four players stand at the end of the channel with a ball each. One red player, (Gladiator), stands in each of the three zones within the channel, and the fourth acts as a goalkeeper. On a signal from the coach, the yellow team attempt to dribble through the zones in the channel. The red players try to pressure the yellow team, and win the ball to kick it out of the playing area. (The red players can only tackle within their own zone). If they get through the last zone they must try and score in the goal. If this happens, the player must return to the beginning and wait for the rest of their team to return.

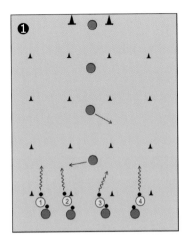

❷ In this diagram, Yellow Player Three has lost possession of their ball and it has been kicked out of the playing area. They must retrieve the ball and go back to the start. Yellow Players One and Two have dribbled through the first two zones and are trying to get through the third to take a shot on goal. Yellow Player Four has dribbled safely through all the zones and is taking a shot on goal.

   All the yellow players return to the start when their turn is over, by going round the sides of the channel. The blue team are then ready to go to try and do the same. Swap another team into the channel zones after two or three rounds, and keep running totals of each team's score.

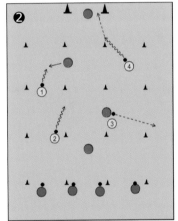

❸ Possible changes

- The coach could act as the goalkeeper, and the teams could each have three players.
- The red players could just apply pressure, and not tackle at first.
- Play with teams of three, with an empty safe zone in the middle of the channel. This will make it easier for the players to get through to take a shot on goal.

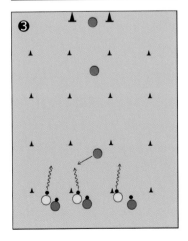

MISSION IMPOSSIBLE

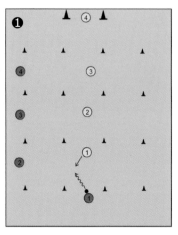

How it works

❶ On a signal from the coach, Red Player One has to try and get past all the yellow defenders and score in the goal at the opposite end of the playing area – Mission Impossible!

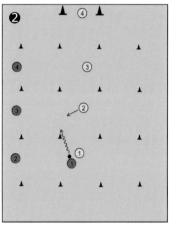

❷ In this diagram, Red Player One has chosen to dribble the ball past Yellow Player One. Each yellow defender is only allowed to challenge for the ball in their section of the channel, marked out by the cones.

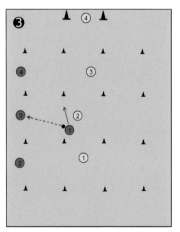

❸ However, Red Player One, has the option of passing the ball to a support player at the side of the channel.

❹ They can then run into the next section to receive a pass back from the same player. The yellow defenders must attempt to tackle the ball and kick it out of the playing area to stop the mission.

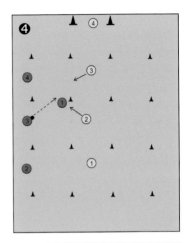

❺ If the red player gets past all the yellow defenders, then they have the chance to complete 'Mission Impossible' by scoring a goal past the goalkeeper.

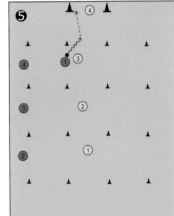

❻ Red Player Two then moves down to the end, to be the next player to take on the mission. All the other red players move down one section of the channel, and Red Player One takes the place of Red Player Five. Yellow Player One then goes to the goalkeeper position, and all the other yellow players move one section down the playing area. Each red player has one attempt to complete 'Mission Impossible' and then the teams swap over, so the yellow players then have their turn. Play as many rounds as you like.

Possible changes
■ Have some, or all, sections of the channel with defenders inside to make it easier or harder.
■ You could also have another team acting as additional support players, on the other side of the channel, if you have larger numbers.
■ Allow red support players to move around inside each section, instead of just standing at the side.

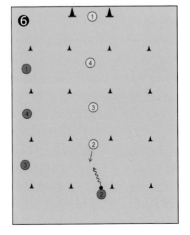

MISSION IMPOSSIBLE 2

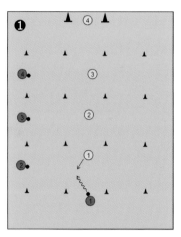

How it works

❶ The set-up is the same as for Mission Impossible. On a signal from the coach, Red Player One has to try and get past all the yellow defenders and score in the goal at the opposite end of the playing area – Mission Impossible!

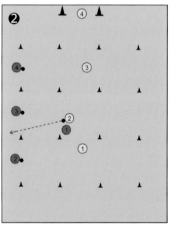

❷ Red Player One has successfully dribbled past Yellow Defender One, but has been tackled by the next defender and the ball has been kicked out.

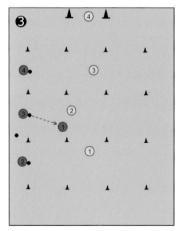

❸ Red Player One can then receive a pass from Red Player Three, and continue on their mission. Yellow Player Two can still attempt to tackle for the ball, until Red Player One has left that section of the playing area.

❹ Red Player One has continued on the mission and successfully dribbled past Yellow Player Three.

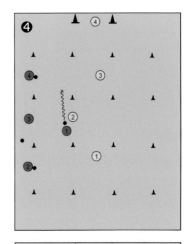

❺ However, Red Player One has been tackled again in section four of the channel, and had to receive another pass from Red Player Five. Yellow Player Four can still attempt to tackle for the ball, until Red Player One has left that section of the playing area.

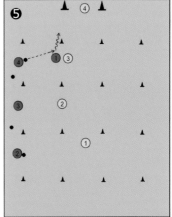

❻ Red Player One can now dribble on to try and score past the yellow player in goal, to complete 'Mission Impossible'. Red Player Two then moves down to the end, to be the next player to take on the mission. All the other red players move down one section of the channel, and Red Player One takes the place of Red Player Five. Yellow Player One then goes to the goal-keeper position, and all the other yellow players move one section down the playing area. Each red player has one attempt to complete 'Mission Impossible', and then the teams swap over so the yellow players then have their turn. Play as many rounds as you like, with the winning team/individual being the one that needed the fewest number of passes.

Possible changes
■ Have some, or all, sections of the channel with defenders inside to make it easier or harder.
■ You could have another team acting as additional support players on the other side of the channel, if you have larger numbers.

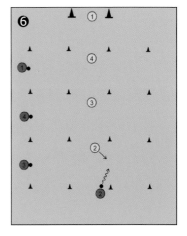

NO MAN'S LAND

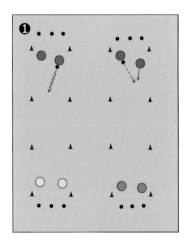

How it works

❶ Pairs of players stand at each end of a channel, with one pair having possession of a ball. Players with the ball can dribble or pass to each other, but only within the end of the three grids in the channel. Place a few spare balls just behind the end of each channel to keep the game flowing.

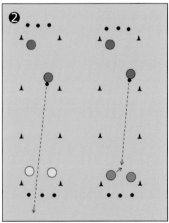

❷ Players are then allowed to take a shot from within their own grid. To score a goal, the ball must pass between the two cones at the other end of the channel, and below the head height of the other team. Players in this team must try to stop the ball from passing through the cones. Allow players to use their hands, or not, as you prefer.

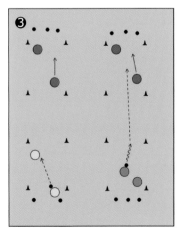

❸ In the left of the channels in this diagram, the yellow team has used a spare ball, after a goal has been scored and passed to their partner to take a shot. In the right of the channels in this diagram, a player in the green team has controlled the ball and is dribbling quickly to the edge of 'No Man's Land' to try and take a shot, before the opposing team are back in position.

 If the ball is not controlled by a player and ends up in 'No Man's Land', then the ball is lost. The other team must then restart the game with a spare ball from behind their end of the channel. Keep score to get a winning team from each game – first to five, or the team in the lead after a four or five-minute time limit. Have a play-off with the winning and losing teams playing against each other, or play a round-robin tournament.

LONG BALL TENNIS

How it works

❶ Pairs of players stand at each end of a channel, with one pair having possession of a ball. Players can dribble or pass to each other, but only within the grid at the end of the channel. Place a few spare balls just behind the end of each channel to keep the game flowing.

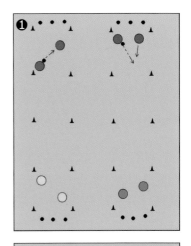

❷ Players pass the ball in the air, to try and land it inside the grid of the opposing team. If the ball lands outside the opponent's grid, then a point goes to the other team. These players must control the ball within their grid, on the full or after a bounce. If they don't control the ball within their grid, then a point goes to the opposition.

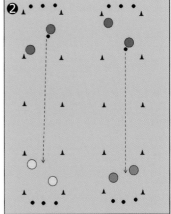

❸ Players have three touches of the ball, to play a lofted pass back into the grid of the other team. Keep score to get a winning team from each game – first to ten points, or the team in the lead after a four or five-minute time limit. Then have a play-off, with winning and losing teams playing against each other.

Possible changes

■ Play a round-robin tournament where all the teams play against each other.
■ Restrict or increase the number of touches, or the size of the grid, depending on the ability of the players.

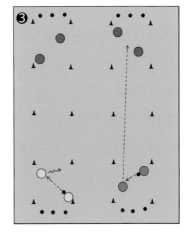

KNOCK OFF 2

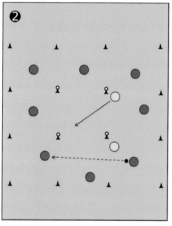

How it works

❶ The red players start with the ball and have to keep possession from the yellow defenders. The red players must stay in their own grid, but the yellow defenders are allowed to move freely from one grid to another.

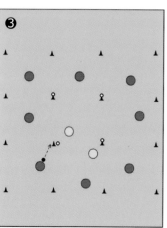

❷ The red players pass the ball between them to try and create an opportunity to score.

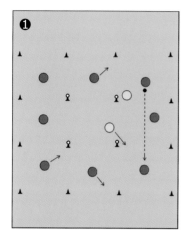

❸ The red team score by knocking a ball off a cone in the centre of the grids. If the red team score, the ball is replaced on top of the cone and play is restarted with a pass from a red player, at the edge of the playing area. If the yellow players intercept the ball, or force a mistake three times, then they swap with two of the red players. Alternatively, allow them to try and knock a ball off to win the game.

Possible changes

- The red team have to complete ten passes before they are allowed to try and knock the ball off the central cone.
- Add a third yellow defender to make it more of a challenge. Add another red player, who stays in the central grid but is only allowed to pass to others, not score.
- Add another ball, to have two in possession at the same time.

SQUARE PASSING

How it works

❶ All the players stand, and must stay, between the cones along the inner sides of the square grids. Player Four has started with the ball and passes to Player One. Player One can then only pass to a player with whom they share the side square, in this case Players Two, Three, Four, Six and Seven.

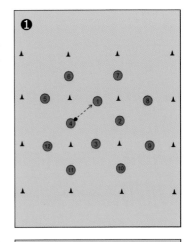

❷ After controlling the ball, Player One chooses to pass to Player Six. Player Six can then only pass to a player with whom they share the side of a square, in this case Players One, Five and Seven. Players continue to pass the ball around to players with whom they share the side of a square. Once the players have got used to the rules, then add another ball and see how long they can keep passes going without any errors. If doing well, then add another ball.

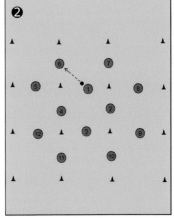

❸ Add in a couple of yellow defenders to apply some pressure to the red team. The defenders are only allowed to intercept a pass, not tackle a red player. How long can the red players keep possession of the balls? Change the defenders and attempt to beat the previous best time, or number of passes.

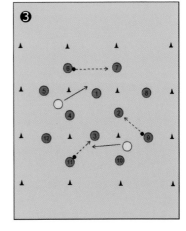

Possible changes

■ Players could also be positioned on the outside edges of the playing area. However, player positions would need to be changed around, as more passes will go through the edges of the central square.

■ If you really want to make it harder, insist that each player touch a cone either side of them, before they are allowed to receive another pass.

BREAKOUT

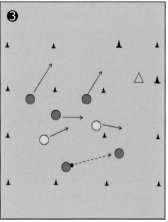

How it works

❶ The red players try to keep possession of the ball from the two yellow defenders. They must keep the ball within the grid area, in the left lower corner of the larger playing area.

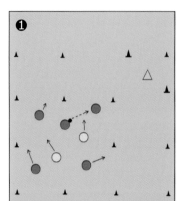

❷ The red players must try to make ten consecutive passes, without losing possession of the ball or knocking it out of the grid. The yellow defenders are only allowed to intercept a pass, not tackle a player in possession. If the yellow players do intercept a pass, or knock the ball out of the grid, then the red players must start again.

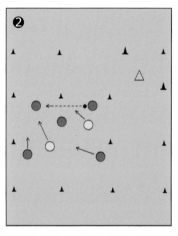

❸ When the red team have completed ten passes, they are allowed to 'Breakout' into the larger playing area, and attempt to score in the top right hand corner goal. Rotate the players so that all take on different roles.

Possible changes

- Allow yellow players to tackle.
- Make it easier by playing four or five versus one, in the small grid, or play five or six versus three, to make it harder.

SQUAREBALL

How it works

❶ The red players are positioned in each of the grids, apart from the one in the centre, but must stay in their own grid. Three yellow players act as defenders, and are allowed to move into any of the grids within the playing area.

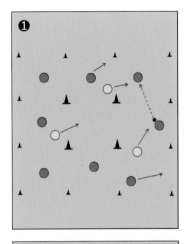

❷ The red players try to keep possession of the ball. They get one point for a pass to a team-mate, within the playing area. If the defenders intercept or tackle the ball and kick it out of the area, then the red players must start their points count again. This also happens if the red players allow the ball to go out of the playing area by mistake.

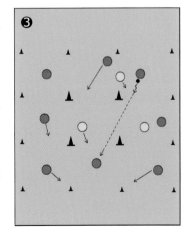

❸ If the red players pass through the central grid, then they get a bonus five points. Play for three or four minutes, attempting to beat previous best scores, and then change the roles of the players.

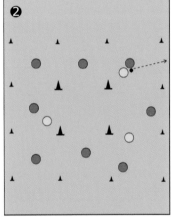

Possible changes

- Play with two yellow defenders to make it easier, or four if you want to make it really difficult.
- Restrict the red players to only two touches on the ball.
- Yellow defenders are only allowed to intercept passes, but not make tackles.

GRIDBALL

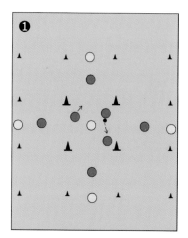

How it works

❶ Three red players attempt to keep possession against one blue defender, inside the central grid.

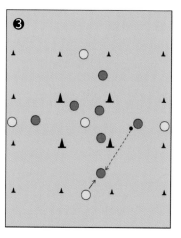

❷ The red players in the central grid are allowed to pass to their team-mates in the other four grids. As soon as the ball is passed into one of these outer grids, a yellow defender can move into the same grid, to pressure the red player in possession.

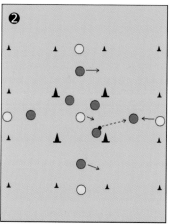

❸ Red players can also pass diagonally from one outer grid to another. As before, the yellow defender can then move into that grid, to pressure the player in possession. The defenders can be passive and just apply pressure, or fully active to intercept and make tackles. Keep challenging the red team to beat the previous best number of passes without an error being made. Play for four or five minutes, then swap roles.

Possible changes

■ Play without the yellow defenders at the outer grids, but allow the yellow player in the centre to move freely around the playing area.

■ Restrict red players to two touches on the ball.

■ Yellow defenders start inside the outer grids, to make it much harder for those players to get free to receive a pass.

THROUGH THE CENTRE

How it works

❶ The red player in the central square of the grids, starts by passing the ball to another red player in the outer playing area. The red player in the central grid can't move out of that area, and the other players are not allowed inside it.

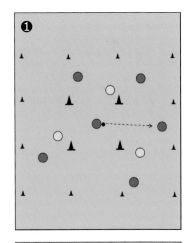

❷ The red players must then try and keep possession of the ball from the yellow defenders. Each pass outside the central square earns the red team a point. They are allowed to make a lofted pass over the central square, to a player on the opposite side of the playing area.

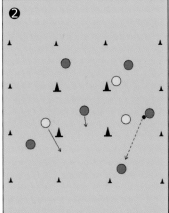

❸ If the red team can pass to the central player, they earn three points for the team. To earn the three points, the ball must first be passed between at least two players in the outer area. If a pass is played straight back from the outer area into the central grid square, it only counts as one point. If the ball goes out of play, restart the game with another pass from the player in the central grid. Play for four or five minutes, trying to beat previous best scores and then change the roles of the players.

Possible changes

■ Make the central square smaller, to give more space in the outer playing area.

■ Make it easier by playing six or seven versus two, or play four or five versus four, in the outer playing area, to make it harder.

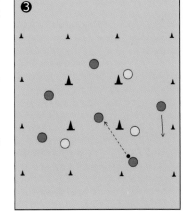

CHAPTER 6

Half-Pitch and Penalty Area Drills

If you have a marked out pitch area, it can make these drills easier to set up, but don't be put off if you don't. Any large open space can be marked out with cones to create the lay-outs used here. Large traffic cones make ideal pieces of training equipment, though they can be a little heavy to carry. They provide the perfect substitute for goal posts, make ideal, very passive defenders and, if placed together, can even double up as a goalkeeper to encourage players to shoot for the corners, or across the face of the goal.

Being creative in ways like this is extremely beneficial when working with groups of different ages and abilities. What works for an Under Eleven team coaching session, on a grassy soccer pitch, will not necessarily be suitable for a class group of thirty, mixed ability boys and girls, on a tarmac playground the size of a postage stamp! You have to be flexible in this game; if something isn't working, then have the confidence to change your plans and try a different approach. Hopefully, provided within the pages of this book, there are enough ideas to help you plan, vary and adapt your coaching sessions for years to come. Then who knows,

you will probably be so full of your own new ideas, you could write a book of your own!

POSSIBLE SESSIONS

The following selections are only suggestions of how drills could be combined to create a one, or two-hour session. As a teacher, or coach, you need to assess the ability of your group and take into account possible numbers, before making appropriate choices of your own. All these sessions could also be started with a warm-up of your own and ended with some regular small-sided games.

- Skill Squares
- Asteroid Blast
- Attack of the Green Goblins (Chapter 2)

- Evan Almighty
- Goal Rush
- Rush Hour

- Mousehunt
- Countdown
- Compete to Score
- Cops and Robbers
- Soccer Cricket

- Heading Race
- Heading Race 2
- Quickfire
- First Touch to Shoot
- Numbers Up

THREE LITTLE PIGS

How it works

❶ All players are 'Little Pigs' and dribble around inside the area, (house of straw), on the edge of the halfway line. The coach is the wolf and comes up to the side of the 'house' and knocks on the door. (Coach calls out: 'Knock, knock, knock'). The players must stop the ball and stand still.

- Coach: 'Little Pigs, little pigs, please let me in.'
- Players: 'Not by the hairs of our chinny, chin, chin.'
- Coach: 'Then I'll huff and I'll puff and I'll blow your house in.'

At this point, the coach gives three really big huffs (blowing over the house of straw). The little pigs must then all dribble into the next area, (house of sticks), before the coach can pick up the two cones and catch any of them. If the coach does catch any of the players, then he 'gobbles them up'.

❷ All the 'Little Pigs' now dribble around inside the next area, (house of sticks). The coach knocks on the door again, repeating the previous sayings from the story. The coach again gives three really big huffs (blowing over the house of sticks). The little pigs must then all dribble into the next area, (house of bricks) before the coach can pick up the two cones and catch any of them and 'gobble them up'.

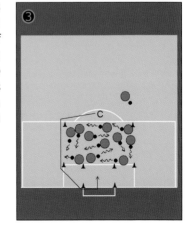

❸ This is then repeated at the house of bricks, but this time the coach, (wolf), can't blow it down. The coach then walks round to the chimney at the other side of the 'house of bricks', accompanied by much squealing panic amongst the 'little pigs'. The players can only stop the wolf by passing the ball to hit them. If the players miss, the only thing they have left to do is try to run away. All these instructions can sound a bit complicated but once the players get the idea, it's great fun!

EVAN ALMIGHTY (NOAH'S ARK)

How it works

❶ Each pair gives themselves the name of an animal, and can make sound effects to fit, if they wish. Pairs of players dribble and pass a ball to each other, within a large area on the edge of the halfway line. At any time, the coach can shout out the names of one or more animals.

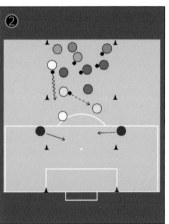

❷ If their animal is called, that pair of players has to try and dribble, or pass, their ball to get to the six-yard box, (the Ark), inside the penalty area. However, they have to get past the two defenders, (ball wreckers, or police, if you've seen the film). If tackled and the ball is kicked out of the playing area, then they have to go back to the large area with all the other animals. The other players can either stop and cheer them on, or carry on passing to each other.

❸ If successful, they can stay safely in the Ark, like the yellow pair in this diagram. The white pair had their ball kicked out, so have to make their way back to the start. Keep playing until the last pair of animals has got to the Ark.

Possible changes

■ If you want to make it competitive, then the last pair to the Ark can drop out and all the other pairs of animals play another round. The pairs who are out could take turns to play the role of the defenders, so they are still involved.

■ Play with one defender and only call several animal pairs at a time, to make it easier to get to the Ark.

GOAL RUSH

How it works

❶ Two equal teams of players each have a ball and dribble around inside a large area, on the edge of the halfway line. The coach can shout out parts of the body and players of both teams have to stop the ball and put that part of their body on the ball.

Unless the coach shouts out: 'Red – knee' or 'Yellow – head', in which case only that colour team stops and follows that instruction.

❷ If the coach shouts: 'Goal Rush', then the yellow team have to dribble their balls towards the goal in an attempt to score. The red team leave their balls where they are and run to try and stop any of the yellow players from scoring. They must tackle the yellow players and kick their ball out of the playing area. If a yellow player has their ball kicked out, they can help another of their team members by being available for a pass to keep possession and try to score.

❸ Keep playing until all the yellow team have either scored, or had their ball kicked out of the playing area. Retrieve the balls and start again, each player dribbling their own ball in the large area on the edge of the halfway line. Play two or three rounds for each team, and keep a tally of the scores to arrive at a winning team.

Possible changes

■ Add a goalkeeper if you wish, but it can be a bit difficult for them if three players are advancing on the goal at the same time.

■ Have the players in the middle and an extra goal on the halfway line. The yellow team must score in one direction, and the reds in the other if called. Or, if you want real chaos, allow them to score in either goal!

SKILL SQUARES

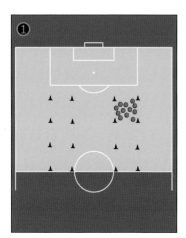

How it works

❶ All players start in one of the four grids, where the coach demonstrates a particular skill. Allow the group a little time to practise. Give the square a number, or the name of a famous soccer player, or club. The skills chosen will depend on the age and ability of the group but here are a few suggestions:

- toe-taps on top of the ball;
- instep touches – stationary or moving around the square;
- roll over the ball with the sole of the foot;
- dribble with drag back turns;
- dribble with Cruyf turns;
- dribble with inside/outside of the foot cuts;
- dribble with step-over;
- pick the ball up, throw it in the air and jump to catch it at the highest point possible;
- keep-ups.

❷ The players then dribble a ball across to another grid, and the coach demonstrates another skill. Repeat this for the other two grids, demonstrating a different skill each time. Even throw in a silly one, like players throwing themselves to the floor and rolling around in agony, screaming as if they have been fouled.

❸ The coach can then randomly call out the number/name of different grids. The players dribble to that grid, as quickly as possible, and perform the skill until the coach calls another one. Keep calling numbers/names, getting quicker as the players become more familiar with the skills. Set a time limit of ten seconds to get from one square to the next, to encourage them to run quickly with the ball, if not already doing so.

ASTEROID BLAST

How it works

❶ Tell the group the story of the films *Armageddon/Deep Impact,* where an asteroid is heading towards Earth and will destroy the planet, unless missiles can blow it up. The balls are the missiles and the goal is the asteroid. Set the group a target they must achieve to save the Earth. Make this first target easily achievable, such as three minutes to impact, or three missiles to destroy the asteroid. On a signal from the coach, Player One in each square has to dribble their ball through each of the other three squares, (in any order), and then stop the ball anywhere between the two cones, in line with the penalty spot.

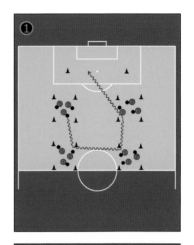

❷ Player One must run back to their square after leaving their ball, (loading their missile), between the cones. As soon as Player One is back in the square, Player Two must do the same, and then Player Three.

❸ When Player Three returns to the square, Player One can prepare to fire their missile at the asteroid, (shoot a ball at the goal). They must run through each of the squares, (in any order), and then run to shoot any ball at the goal. Hit or miss, they must run back to their square so that Player Two can do the same, and then Player Three. The game is not over until the last Player Three has shot their missile at the asteroid. Retrieve the balls and get each group to move round to start from a different square. Set a harder target and play again.

Possible changes

■ When firing the missiles, the players could run straight to the ball to shoot, rather than having to run through each square.

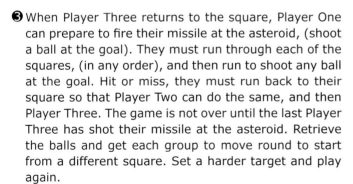

RUSH HOUR

How it works

❶ Four teams of players line up as seen in the diagram. On a signal from the coach, all the players dribble the ball towards the middle grid.

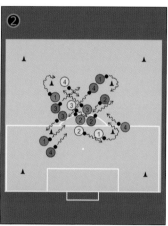

❷ All the players have to dribble towards, and around, the far diagonal cone from where they started. Players must be careful and keep their heads up, whilst dribbling across the central area.

❸ After rounding the far diagonal cone, the players must dribble back to their starting position.

Possible changes

■ Players dribble around the nearest cone, or even all the cones, before returning to their starting position.

■ Players can jog/run around these cones to begin with to get warmed up, or to become familiar with the movement patterns.

■ Players stop their ball inside the central area and then run around one or more of the cones. They can then take any ball and dribble it back to their starting position.

RUNAROUND

How it works

❶ Four teams of players line up, as seen in the diagram. On a signal from the coach, Player Ones dribble the ball towards the cone in the centre of the middle grid.

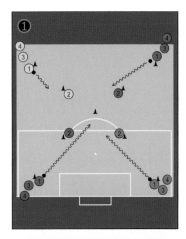

❷ Once around the centre cone they pass to Player Twos and then follow the pass.

❸ Player Twos then dribble the ball back to Player Three who starts the sequence off again.

   Play as a race to get through the whole team one or two times.

Possible changes

■ Allow players to kick their opponent's ball away whilst in the middle grid, especially if behind in the race. If their ball is kicked away, then the player must dribble it back into the middle grid before continuing.

■ Player Twos pass back to Player Threes and follow their pass.

■ Player Ones performs a one-two with Player Twos, before dribbling to the centre cone.

RUNAROUND 2

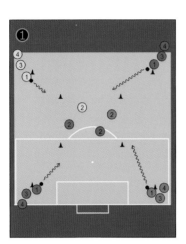

How it works

❶ Four teams of players line up, as seen in the diagram. On a signal from the coach, Player Ones dribble the ball towards the middle grid.

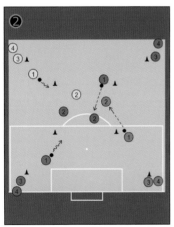

❷ Player Ones pass to Player Twos, when they get to the side of the grid.

❸ Player Twos then have to dribble the ball around any corner cone. Player Ones move inside the grid, ready to receive a pass back from Player Twos. Once Player Twos pass to Player Ones, they must sprint back and tag Player Threes. Player Threes must get into the grid ready to receive a pass from Player Ones, who have had to dribble around a corner cone.

THREE BALL BASEBALL

How it works

❶ On a signal from the coach, the red players, (batters), pass their ball into the playing area. The ball must be kicked in front of them, in a line between first and third base.

    The yellow players, (fielders), can stand anywhere in the playing area, as long as they are in front of first and third base.

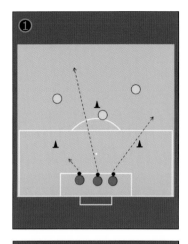

❷ The red players must then set off to run around all the bases, to try and get back to the six-yard area. The yellow players have to run after a ball each and then try and dribble it as quickly as possible, to stop it inside the penalty D. When the first yellow player has stopped a ball inside the penalty D, the others in the team could pass their ball to be controlled and stopped by that player.

❸ In this diagram, the yellow player is just about to dribble the last ball into the penalty D to stop the game. The red team would score as follows:

- four points for a player getting back to the six-yard area;
- three points for a player passing third base;
- two points for a player passing second base.

Change the teams round and play several innings, keeping a running total to arrive at a winner. If you have a large group, then mix the teams up and play as a round-robin competition.

Possible changes

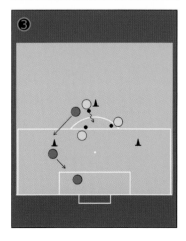

- Allow the fielders to take the risk of trying to run out a batter, by passing the ball to hit the cone they are running towards, before they get to it. The whole team, or just that player, could then be run out and get no score for that inning.

SOCCER CRICKET

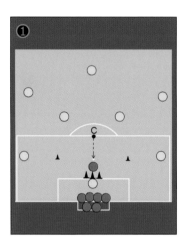

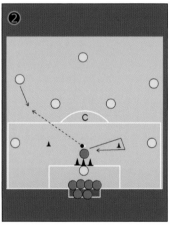

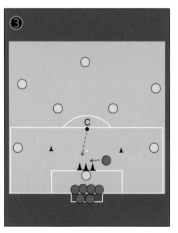

How it works

❶ The coach passes the ball to the first red batter who stands in front of the three cones, (the wickets). If the batter misses the ball and a cone is hit, then the batter is out and the next red player comes in to bat. The batter only has one touch to kick the ball in front of the wickets.

❷ Once the batter has kicked the ball, they have to run around one of the small cones and back to the wickets. The fielding team have to get the ball back to the coach as quickly as possible. The coach must stay in the D on the edge of the penalty area. The batter can run around the small cones more than once if they kick the ball far enough, or the fielding team make a mistake. Score one run for each time a player gets round a cone and back to the wickets.

❸ The coach can pass the ball to hit the wickets as soon as they have the ball at their feet – they do not have to wait for the batter to get back to the wickets! As before, if a cone is knocked down before the batter returns to the wickets, then they are out and the next red player comes in to bat. A batter can also be caught out if one of the fielding team gets a touch on the ball with any part of their body, (apart from hands), before it hits the ground. Play until all the batters are out and then swap the teams over.

HEADING RACE

How it works

❶ Two teams of players line up, as seen in the diagram, with one player standing by each cone outside the penalty area. On a signal from the coach, a stopwatch is started and Player Ones run to the balls and dribble one back to the same cone. As soon as they get back to the cones, Player Ones pick the ball up. They then throw it up in the air and try to head the ball into the hands of Player Two. The players repeat this all the way down the diagonal cones to Player Six, each one heading the ball out of their own hands. If a player drops the ball, they must dribble it back to their cone, before picking it up and heading it to the next player.

❷ Player Six then drops the ball and shoots for goal. The shot must be taken from behind the line of the penalty spot. After shooting at goal they must run back up to the halfway line to collect another ball. Meanwhile, all the other players must move one diagonal place closer to the goal.

❸ Red Player Six has already collected a ball and headed it to Player Two. Yellow Player Six still has to collect and dribble a ball to the first cone, before starting the relay down the cones. The race continues until Player Ones have had a shot on goal, so that every player has had a turn. Each team gets five seconds knocked off their time for each goal they score. Teams can then race off against each other again, but also try to beat the record time set.

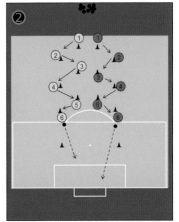

Possible changes

■ Players can just dribble and pass between the cones.
■ Player Ones feed the ball for Player Two, to direct a header for Player Three to catch. Player Threes then feed the ball for Player Four, to direct a header to Player Five to catch. Player Fives then feed the ball for Player Six to head towards goal and shoot.

HEADING RACE 2

How it works

❶ Two teams of players line up, as seen in the diagram, with one player standing by each cone outside the penalty area. On a signal from the coach, a stopwatch is started and Player Ones run to the balls and dribble one back to the same cone. As soon as they get back to the cones, Player Ones pick the ball up. They then throw it up in the air and try to head the ball into the hands of Player Two.

❷ When Player One has headed the ball to Player Two, they must run around the outside of that player, to get ready at the next free cone for a header from Player Three. When Player Two has headed the ball to Player Three, they must run around the outside of that player, to get ready at the next free cone for a header from Player One. If a player drops the ball, they must dribble it back to their cone before picking it up and heading it to the next player. This sequence continues until Player One gets to the last cone.

❸ Player One then drops the ball and shoots for goal. The shot must be taken from behind the line of the penalty spot. Meanwhile, the other players can run back to the halfway line and Player Two can collect a ball to start the sequence again. After shooting at goal, Player One must run back up to the next cone to be ready for their header. The race continues until each player has had two or three shots on goal. Each team gets five seconds knocked off their time for each goal that they score. Teams can then race off against each other again, but also try to beat the record time set.

Possible changes

■ Players can just dribble and pass between the cones.

COPS AND ROBBERS

How it works
❶ Red players are the Cops and must stand in the penalty area, but are not allowed in the six-yard box. Yellow players are the Robbers and must stand in the
centre circle. On a signal from the coach, players from
both teams are allowed to run into the playing area.

❷ The Cops, (red players), try to tag the Robbers, (yellow players). If tagged, the Robber must return to the
centre circle before they can come out again and back
into the game.
   A Robber must try and get into the six-yard box
without being tagged, to gain possession of a ball.

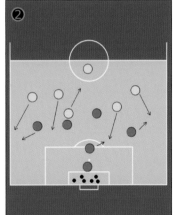

❸ Cops then play against Robbers in a six versus six
game. Robbers must pass or dribble the ball into the
centre circle, (Hideout), and stop it there. Cops must
try to win possession and pass or dribble the ball back
into the six-yard box, (Bank). If the ball goes out at the
side of the playing area, then re-start with a throw-in
to the appropriate team. If the ball goes out at either
end, then it is lost, and the Robbers have to try and
steal another. They can do this as soon as the ball is
lost, without having to return to the centre circle unless they are tagged. Set a time limit of ten minutes
for the Robbers to steal as many balls as possible and
then switch teams.

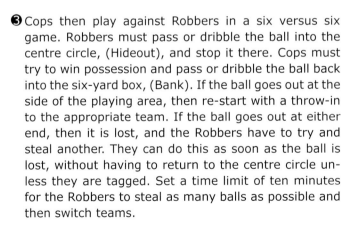

Possible changes
■ Have more Robbers than Cops to make it easier to
steal the balls, and play in a smaller area if you
have less than twelve players.

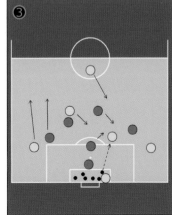

QUIDDITCH

How it works

❶ Play two teams against each other in the area shown. (Place cones to complete a semi-circle with the penalty area D). Have either a ball balanced on the top of a large cone, or a raised target of some kind, at each end of the playing area. Nominate one player on each team to be the 'Seeker' (S). The Seeker is allowed to play in the game, but are the only players who will be allowed to touch the Snitch. Play normal rules, but players are allowed to pick the ball up and pass/shoot with their hands when inside the semi-circle, at either end of the playing area. Score by hitting the ball off the cone, or passing the ball through a raised hoop, or at some kind of target.

❷ At any time during the game the coach shouts 'Snitch' and passes a different coloured ball into the playing area. The two Seekers must then compete for the ball and try to win the game outright, by hitting the ball off the cone, or passing the ball through the raised hoop or other target but are not allowed to pick the ball up.

❸ If successful the game is instantly won, but, if not, the game continues with other goals being scored in normal play. The coach can play the Snitch in again at any time. If the game has not been won outright after five or ten minutes, then the Seeker can be changed if you wish.

Possible changes

■ When the Snitch is played in by the coach, the other players can either continue playing with the normal ball, or stop and cheer on their Seeker.

■ Play any number of players on each team, but you may need to increase the size of the playing area. If the numbers are larger you could have two Seekers on each team to compete for the Snitch, two versus two.

SHOOTOUT AT THE OK CORRAL

How it works

❶ The two goals must be of equal size and the balls placed the same distance away.

Players get together to make pairs. One player is the shooter and their partner is the goalkeeper at the other end. On a signal from the coach, both players by the middle cone run to take their first shot at goal.

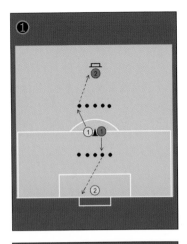

❷ The players must run back to touch the central cone after each shot, before running in to take another shot on goal. Both players need to be timed to see how long it takes them to shoot each of the five balls, and get back to touch the central cone. For each ball missed, however, five or ten seconds is added to the time for that player. The time added will depend on the distance between the two goals.

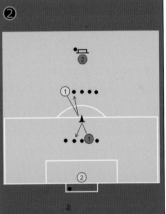

❸ Partners then swap roles and play again. Add the times of both players to arrive at a winning pair. Play as a knock-out game, the winners going through to the next round, or as a best time wins.

Possible changes

■ Play as an individual challenge with neutral goalkeepers.
■ Use as many balls as you like, and for younger players, place the balls closer to the two goals.

COUNTDOWN

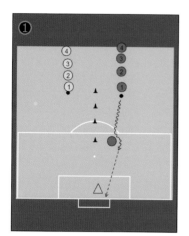

How it works

❶ On a signal from the coach, Red Player One dribbles towards the goal. Other players start the 'Countdown' by calling out the numbers, from ten down to zero. Red Player One has until the countdown reaches zero to score, or at least make an attempt on goal.

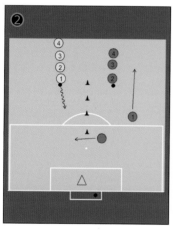

❷ If the red player scores within the time limit, then the coach makes another signal immediately and the Countdown starts again for Yellow Player One. The blue defender must get across to the other side of the penalty area as quickly as possible, to challenge for the ball. The red player goes back to join the line.

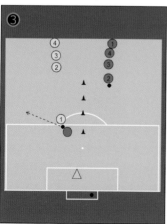

❸ Here, the blue defender has tackled Yellow Player One, and so the countdown starts again immediately for Red Player Two. If a player is held up by the blue defender, running out of time, the countdown starts again for the next player in the other team.

It is up to the coach to give the signals quickly for the next player to start and the new countdown to begin. Keep the scores for a few rounds and then change the defender and goalkeeper if desired.

Possible changes

■ Both Player Ones work as a pair, with a ball between them, to try and score within the ten-second countdown.
■ Increase/decrease the starting distance from the goal, or the amount of seconds in the countdown.
■ Play without a defender to make it easier.

TURN AND SHOOT

How it works
❶ Two teams of players line up, as shown in the diagram, with one player standing by the cone just outside the edge of the penalty area. Red player Two passes the ball to Red Player One.

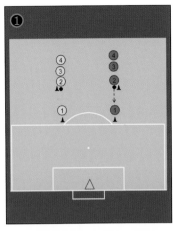

❷ Red Player One has one touch to turn with the ball, and must then shoot with their next touch on the ball. As soon as the red player has taken the shot, Yellow Player Two passes the ball to Yellow Player One, who performs the same skill. Encourage players to turn both ways and shoot with left and right feet accordingly. If a player turns to their right, they should shoot with their left foot, and if a player turns to their left, they should shoot with their right foot. Keep a running total of goals scored with the correct touches, and swap the lines over after two or three rounds. Challenge the group to score a number of goals from so many attempts.

❸ **Possible changes**
■ Red Player One starts with the ball and passes to Red Player Two. Red Player Two passes the ball in behind Red Player One. The ball can be played to either side. Red Player One then turns to shoot, first time, for goal. As soon as Red Player One has taken the shot, Yellow Player One passes to Yellow Player Two to repeat the drill from the other side. Keep running totals, swap lines, or create challenges for the group as outlined earlier.
■ Allow more touches on the ball for younger, or less able, groups or individuals.
■ Change the angle of the pass from Player Twos.

COMPETE TO SCORE

How it works

❶ The coach stands behind Player Ones with a supply of balls, and both players facing the goal. The coach passes the ball between the two players.

❷ As soon as Players Ones see the ball, they react to run forward and compete to win possession. If Player One wins the ball they try to score, whilst Player Two tries to tackle or apply pressure to Player One. If Player Two wins the ball, then they try to score. Have one goalkeeper if you have an odd number, or two goalkeepers who can keep switching if you have an even number. They could swap with another pair after one or two rounds, if you want everyone to have a go in goal. Players can compete for several rounds against the same partner, or switch partners and compete as two teams.

❸ The coach can favour a player with the pass, if they have not got to the ball first after two or three rounds.

Possible changes

- The coach can vary the feed, such as a bouncing ball or high throw in the air.
- Players could start in different positions, such as facing the coach, sitting, kneeling on all fours, lying down and so on, (the sillier, the better!)

COMPETE TO SCORE 2

How it works

❶ Two teams line up on the goal line, at the edge of the six-yard area. The coach throws a ball over the goal and the first player from each team runs out to compete for the ball.

❷ In this diagram, the yellow player has got to the ball first, so they become the attacker. They must try and turn and get a shot on goal. The red player must try to stop the yellow player from shooting and, if possible, win the ball in a tackle.

❸ If this happens, the red player becomes the attacker and the yellow player tries to defend. Allow twenty or thirty seconds for one of the players to get a shot on goal, or score. The coach then throws out another ball for the next player from each team. Keep a running total of the team scores. The coach can favour one of the players with the throw, if they have not got to the ball first after a couple of rounds.

Possible changes

■ As with 'Compete to Score', the players could be asked to start in different positions.
■ The coach could also be the goalkeeper.
■ The players in each team could also be given a number. The coach then calls the number(s) of one or more players, to run out and compete to score.

COMPETE TO SCORE 3

How it works

❶ Two teams line up on the goal line, at the edge of the six-yard area. On a signal from the coach, the first player in each team runs out to go around the cone and turn back towards the goal.

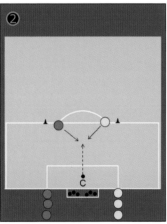

❷ As the two players round the cone, the coach rolls a ball out into the middle of the penalty area. The two players compete to get to the ball first.

❸ If the coach makes a save and the ball rebounds back into play, then the game continues until a goal is scored, or the ball goes out of the playing area. The coach then gives another signal for the next player from each team to go. The coach can favour one of the players with the throw, if they have not got to the ball first after a couple of rounds. Keep a running total of the team scores, but swap the teams to the opposite sides of the goal to make it fair.

Possible changes

■ The coach can vary the feed, such as a bouncing ball or a high throw.
■ Players can start in different positions as with the other 'Compete to score' drills.
■ The two teams can start in different places, such as the corners of the penalty area.

MOUSE HUNT

How it works

❶ The red players are mice and have a bib/pinny stuck down the back of their shorts, (mouse tail). The yellow players are the Mouse Hunters. On a signal from the coach, the red players, (mice), come out of the goal and can run free, anywhere in the penalty area. The yellow players, (Mouse Hunters), can catch a mouse by removing the bib/pinny from their shorts, (pinching the tail). The red player, (mouse), then has to return to stand inside the goal (Mouse trap).

❷ When one or more mice are caught, a ball, (piece of cheese), can be taken from the edge of the penalty area. The red players can dribble with the ball, or pass to each other, to try and get the ball into the goal. If they succeed, all the mice in the goal are set free. They must remember to put their bib/pinny back in their shorts. The yellow players try to stop them getting the ball into the goal. If they kick the ball out of the penalty area, then it cannot be used again. There are three balls that the mice can use altogether, so they must think about how best to use them. When all the balls are gone, then the Mouse Hunters just have to catch the rest of the mice.

❸ In this diagram, the yellow player has kicked one of the balls out of the playing area, so a different red player is going towards another ball, in an attempt to free the other mice. The game ends when all the mice are back in the trap. Time how long it takes to get all the mice back in the trap, and challenge another pair of Mouse Hunters to do better. Could the mice have used the balls more effectively, by waiting until more mice are in the trap?

Possible changes

■ The game can be played as a straightforward chase and catch, without the balls on the edge of the penalty area.

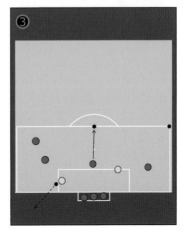

CUPPY

How it works

❶ We used to play this game when I was at school and I loved it. When we played there were often up to twenty of us at any one time, but I would not recommend any more than twelve, as an absolute maximum. The coach, (or a goalkeeper if you have an odd number of players), stands in the goal with a supply of balls and throws one up in the air, for all the teams to try and gain possession and shoot on goal.

❷ At this stage, players have to shoot quickly as the area is crowded, so encourage them to take first-time shots. If a shot by the blue player hits a green player before going in, then the goal is awarded to the green team.

❸ When a team scores a goal, they are through to the next round of the Cup, standing behind the goal out of the way. As the number of teams reduces, a little more passing is possible between team-mates. The team who are left, without scoring a goal, are then out of the Cup and all the other teams are back in to compete in the next round. When only two teams are left in the final, they play first to score three goals to win the Cup.

Possible changes

■ You could have four teams of three, with a group of twelve, or play two teams at a time as semi-finals. You could then have a third and fourth place final, and a first and second place final, just as they do in the World Cup.

■ As children we also used to play it individually, if there weren't that many of us, but it could sometimes take a while, with players sitting out for long periods.

QUICK FIRE

How it works

❶ Numbered pairs of players stand on the edge of the penalty area D, both facing towards the goal. If you've got an odd number of players, then use one of them as a goalkeeper, but if you've got an even number then the coach could go in goal. The red players have a ball at their feet and the yellow players stand with their legs open.

❷ When their number is called by the coach, the red player passes the ball between the yellow player's legs, for them to run on to and take a shot on goal. As soon as the shot has been taken, the coach then calls another number for that pair to do the same.

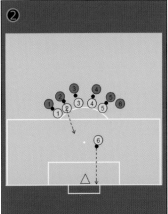

❸ Quickly go through each pair and then reverse roles. Teams can compete against each other, with the number of goals scored in a certain number of rounds.

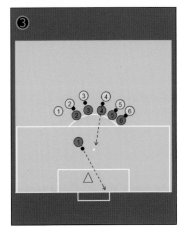

Possible changes

- ■ Younger players can roll the ball between their partner's legs.
- ■ Yellow players face away from the goal to turn and shoot.
- ■ Red players throw the ball over the yellow player's heads, for them to run on to and strike on the volley/half-volley.
- ■ The coach shouts two numbers. The first number gets the ball passed through their legs to attempt to score, whilst the second number tries to apply pressure, or even make a tackle.

HIT THE TARGET

How it works

❶ The coach stands behind a goalkeeper, with a good supply of balls in the goal. At any time the coach can roll or kick the ball between the goalkeeper's legs. Red Player One then makes a move towards the ball.

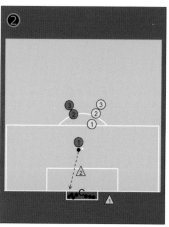

❷ Red Player One can take a controlling touch if desired. The player must then attempt to score by shooting past, or dribbling around, the goalkeeper. Red Player One then goes to the back of the line and the drill is repeated for Red Players Two and Three.

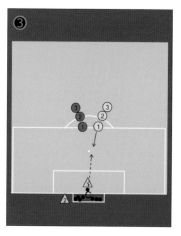

❸ The goalkeepers then swap over and the drill is repeated for all the yellow players. The two teams compete against each other to score the most goals, or the goalkeepers compete to see who can prevent the most goals, over several rounds.

Possible changes

■ Goalkeepers face the coach and have to turn, after the ball has been rolled between their legs. The goalkeepers could also start kneeling or lying down, standing outside a post, or in any other position, as the coach rolls a ball into play.

■ Players must shoot directly on goal with their first touch.

FIRST TOUCH TO SHOOT

How it works

❶ Two lines of players stand either side of the coach, at the edge of the penalty area.

   The first red player stands facing the coach and side-on to the goal. The coach passes the ball in to the feet of the red player.

❷ The red player controls the ball with their right foot, through the cone gate and into the penalty area, where they take a shot on goal.

❸ The coach then turns and plays a ball into the feet of the yellow player, who takes it on their left foot, through the cone gate and shoots on goal. Swap players to the other side after a few rounds, and you can make it more competitive by keeping scores.

Possible changes

■ One touch through the cone gate and first-time shot only.

■ When the red player enters the penalty area to shoot, have the first yellow player follow in to take advantage of any rebounds.

■ Do the same, but have the yellow player acting as a defender to add extra pressure.

■ The coach feeds the ball in the air for the player to control first, or for their controlling touch to take them through the cone gate.

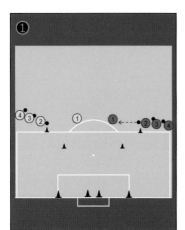

FIRST TOUCH TO SHOOT 2

How it works

❶ Two lines of players stand behind a cone, at either side of the penalty area. Red and Yellow Player Ones stand on the edge of the penalty area D, and side-on to the goal. Red Player Two passes the ball to Red Player One.

❷ Red Player One has one touch to play the ball towards the goal, and must then shoot with their second touch. Points are awarded to the players as follows:

■ Three points for a shot scoring in either corner of the goal;

■ Two points for a shot scoring in the centre of the goal;

■ One point for a shot going in between the goalpost and the cone placed at the edge of the six-yard area.

The shot must be taken before the ball passes the cones inside the penalty area, or no points are scored. These can be placed closer, or further away from the goal, depending on age and ability. As soon as Red Player One has taken a shot, Yellow Player Two passes the ball to Yellow Player One for them to do the same.

❸ Red Player One collects the ball and dribbles back to the edge of the penalty area to re-join the line. Yellow Player One gains two points for scoring in the central part of the goal. Red Player Two has moved into position on the edge of the penalty area D, to receive a pass from Red Player Three. The coach needs to keep the practise moving so that players are not standing around in lines for any length of time. Swap the lines over from one side of the goal to the other, and take an equal number of shots from each side. Players can compete individually to gain the most points and/or as a team.

Possible changes

■ Restrict the players to using only left or right foot for the first touch, and/or the shot from the correct side of the goal.

■ Add a goalkeeper if desired.

MAKE YOUR MOVE

How it works

❶ The red attacker and yellow defender stand just behind the penalty spot. Other pairs of players stand by the goal, ready to come into the playing area. The coach has a supply of balls to keep the drill flowing. Firstly, the coach passes the ball in to the feet of the red player.

❷ The red player has to try and 'make a move', such as: fake to go one way and then touch the ball out of their feet in the other direction, to gain space between them and the yellow defender. The red player can make their move towards either goal.

❸ The red player then attempts to shoot on goal. Pairs of players rotate into the playing area. Reverse roles so the yellow players become the attackers, and also change goalkeepers after a few rounds. The defender can be passive at first and then become more active, depending on the age and ability of the players. You can make it more competitive by keeping team scores.

Possible changes

- First touch and shoot only.
- Coach can feed the ball in the air.
- If the yellow player wins the ball, then they can try and score in the opposite goal.

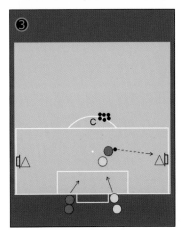

PERFECT HAT TRICK

How it works

❶ Sometimes ideas for drills come from an odd variety of places. This one came from watching a Saturday morning television programme called *Soccer AM*. Whilst showing the best goals from the week's games, occasionally they would highlight a player scoring the 'perfect hat trick'. The 'perfect hat trick' is only completed when a goal is scored with each foot, and one with a header. The red player makes a run into the penalty area to receive a pass from the coach.

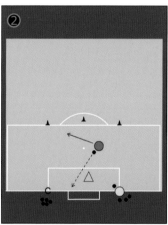

❷ The red player shoots for goal first time, with no touch to control the ball. After hitting the shot, the red player must make a run to the cone at the other side of the penalty area. The yellow player gets a ball ready to feed in for the next shot.

❸ After touching the top of the cone, the red player turns and makes another run back into the penalty area to receive a pass from the yellow player. The coach gets a ball ready to feed in for the final header.

❹ The red player shoots for goal first time, with no touch to control the ball. After hitting the shot, the red player must make a run to the cone in the middle of the penalty area D.

❺ After touching the top of the cone, the red player turns and makes another run back into the penalty area to receive a thrown feed from the coach.

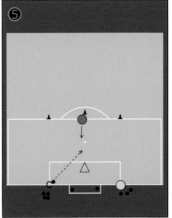

❻ The red player heads for goal first time, with no touch to control the ball, to complete the 'Perfect Hat trick'. The red player then swaps with the yellow player to repeat the practise.

Possible changes
- Include a passive defender, to add pressure from behind the striker, when attempting to score.
- Include a feed in the air, for the striker to volley into the goal.
- Allow a controlling touch before each shot.

NUMBERS UP

How it works

❶ Red players one to four, stand around the edge of the penalty area with a ball at their feet.

Two red and yellow players stand inside the penalty area with a neutral goalkeeper.

The coach shouts a number and that player can either move into the penalty area with the ball, or pass it in to another red player. In this diagram Player Three has been called by the coach and has passed the ball to another red player.

❷ Player Three has now moved into the penalty area to make it a three versus two game. Another player must touch the ball before Player Three is allowed to score. The red players try and pass and move to create a scoring opportunity. Red players earn one point for every goal they score.

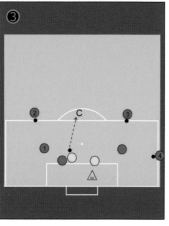

❸ The yellow players act as defenders to try and prevent this from happening. If they win possession of the ball they can kick it out of the penalty to play safe, or pass to the coach within the penalty area D to earn a point. Play ten times, keeping score and then change roles.

Possible changes

■ Start with three versus three in the penalty area to make it harder for the attackers, or start with two or three versus one if you want to make it easier.

■ The yellow players change to being the attackers straight away, if they pass the ball to the coach.

SHOOTOUT

How it works

❶ Each player in the line has a ball, with a supply of spare balls close by to keep the drill flowing. On a signal from the coach, both Player Twos pass the ball in to the feet of Player Ones.

❷ Player One controls the ball and shoots at goal. After taking their shot, Player One runs to the back of their line and Player Two runs out to the cone between the goals.

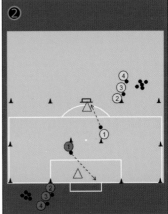

❸ Player Three then passes a ball for Player Two to control and shoot at goal. Teams can compete against each other by being the first to score five or ten goals, or by scoring the most goals in a set period of time.

Possible changes

- Teams can move to the other side of the goal for another round.
- Players run to the opposite line as soon as they have taken their shot, and players just keep rotating in this way. Challenge the whole group to then score a set number of goals, within a certain time limit.
- Restrict players to one controlling touch or to shoot first time.

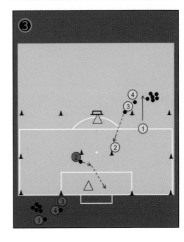

SHOOTOUT 2

How it works

❶ Each player in the line has a ball, with a supply of spare balls close by to keep the drill flowing. On a signal from the coach, both Player Twos pass the ball in to the feet of Player Ones.

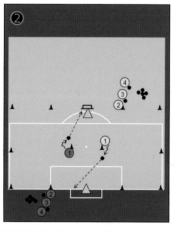

❷ Player Ones turn and shoot on goal.

❸ As soon as Player One has taken the shot, Player Two moves to the central cone and receives a pass from Player Three to turn and shoot. Player One returns to the back of the line. Teams can compete against each other by being the first to score five or ten goals, or by scoring the most goals in a set period of time.

Possible changes

■ Teams can move to the other side of the goal for another round.

■ Restrict to one touch to turn and first-time shot.

■ Player One makes a move towards Player Two, before turning away to the goal.

■ Player Two passes the ball in behind Player One for a first time shot on goal.

DIAGONAL PASS AND SHOOT

How it works

❶ Red Player One passes the ball across the penalty area to Red Player Five. As soon as Red Player Five touches the ball, Yellow Player Three is allowed to enter the penalty area as a defender.

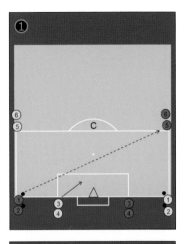

❷ Red Player Five has to try and get a shot on goal before the defender can get in a position to make a challenge. Players return to the back of the same line that they came from.

❸ Repeat the drill with Yellow Player One passing the ball diagonally across the penalty area to Yellow Player Five. Rotate player positions after a few rounds, and you could make it more competitive by keeping scores.

Possible changes

■ Allow Player One to enter the penalty area after making the pass, to make it two versus one players against the defender.

■ With younger players, the coach could pass the ball to Red Player Five, and then Red Player One and Yellow Player Three could enter the penalty area to play two versus one.

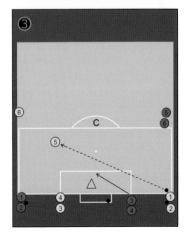

Index